Milan & the Italian Lakes

Berlitz®

Milan & the Italian Lakes

Text by Patricia Schultz
Edited by Media Content Marketing, Inc.
Photography: Chris Coe
Cover photograph by Jon Davison
Layout: Media Content Marketing, Inc.
Cartography by Raffaele De Gennaro
Managing Editor: Tony Halliday

Tenth Edition 2002

Contacting the Editors

Every effort has been made to provide accurate information in this publication, but changes are inevitable. The publisher cannot be responsible for any resulting loss, inconvenience or injury. We would appreciate it if readers would call our attention to any errors or outdated information by contacting Berlitz Publishing, PO Box 7910, London SE1 1WE, England. Fax: (44) 20 7403 0290;
e-mail: berlitz@apaguide.demon.co.uk

Printed in Singapore by Insight Print Services (Pte) Ltd, 38 Joo Koon Road, Singapore 628990. Tel: (65) 6865-1600. Fax: (65) 6861-6438

090/210 REV

CONTENTS

NATO IN VINCI DI VALDARNO
GIO ANTONIO
LUNGAMENTE OSPITE INVIDIATO

- A ☛ in the text denotes a highly recommended sight

Milan

PIZZERIA TRADIZIONALE
MESCITA DI VINI FINI

MILAN AND THE MILANESE

Milan is located in the Po Valley in the northwest of Italy, separated by the Alps from the mighty cultural and commercial powers of Germany and France. As capital of Lombardy, it shares the valley with the university town of Pavia; hilltop Bergamo, stylish outpost of the Venetian Empire; and, on the way east to Lake Garda, the lively industrial city of Brescia. It is just 50 km (30 miles) south of the Swiss border.

By rights, for its energy, style, and economic power, Milan should be the capital of Italy. To get a feel for Italian creativity today, for better and for worse, this is the place to be. In industry, fashion, and commerce, the city sets both tastes and standards for the whole country and much of Europe as well.

Although elegant and industrious, vibrant and forward-looking, Milan can in no way challenge Rome's claim on the popular imagination. Other than a few Corinthian columns at the old Porta Ticinese town gate, it lacks any substantial links with the ancient classical world. What's more, despite the presence of Leonardo da Vinci and the splendid art collection of the Brera and other museums, the city remained peripheral to the major achievements of the Renaissance era.

Although Napoleon conquered many great cities around Europe, only Milan thought of erecting a statue of him in the nude, right in front of the Brera Museum. Among 19th-century edifices, the Galleria Vittorio Emanuele is not just another shopping arcade, but an eloquent tribute to the industrial age of steel and glass. Then there is La Scala opera house: unprepossessing as it may look from the outside, in its interior and sublime prestige it stands as a monument of quasi-sacred dimensions throughout the world.

Moving forward, the city's 1920s railway station, the monumental and imposing Stazione Centrale, is an apt expression of Mussolini's questionable version of the modern age. The graceful Pirelli skyscraper directly opposite makes an aesthetically interesting contrast.

If all this modernity gets to be too much, you can always wander away from it with a stroll along the 16th-century Navigli canals by the Porta Ticinese gate or in the gardens behind the Castello Sforzesco.

Living in Style

Milan's strategic location as a gateway between northern Europe and Italy attracted many invaders, notably the Spanish, the French, and the Austrians. It was the Austrians of the 19th-century Hapsburg Empire, however, who left the most visible mark. There is more than a distinctive touch of Vienna in the sweep of ring roads around the old city center *(centro storico)* and broad avenues lined with imposing Neo-Classical buildings.

One of many remarkably detailed statues that adorn the Duomo.

Style is an essential part of the Milan ethos, and nowhere is it more apparent than in the exclusive shops on and around Via Montenapoleone. Here, the pure genius of Italian design, whether it be in fashion or coffee pots, furniture or fountain pens, comes into its own.

Similar detailing goes into the cuisine of the city's many excellent restaurants, which benefit from the freshest produce of the rich surrounding farmlands of the Po Valley. Look for Milanese specialties such as the classic *osso bucco* with saffron-scented risotto.

The grandiose Duomo is an integral element of the city.

The Milanese themselves are a hard-working bunch. One third of the city's population of 1.5 million (of which very few are actually native to the city) is employed in industry, and the Milanese in general who account for scarcely 3 percent of the national population contribute one quarter of Italy's total income-tax revenues.

"La Dolce Vita"

The attraction of Milan lies not just in the city itself – there is also the bonus of the surrounding countryside. Leave the city

Music is in the air in Milan. These two buskers peddle their melodies on Via Dante.

behind and escape to the lakes, a world apart where the waters lap the foothills of the Alps.

Italy's famous trio of elongated lakes—Maggiore, Como, and Garda—constitutes one of Europe's most romantic resort areas. Here you'll also find outstanding art museums in Bergamo and Brescia and, south of Milan, the Carthusian monastery of Certosa di Pavia—a jewel of late Gothic and Renaissance art. With vineyards, groves of orange and olive trees, atmospheric mists, craggy cliffs, and brilliant sun, the lakes are a home away from home for the poet, painter, and lover in us all.

A BRIEF HISTORY

Milan's first settlement was founded in 600 B.C. as the capital of the Insubres, a Celtic tribe from Gaul. It was known as *Mediolanum,* "town at the center"—legend also goes that it was named after a half-woolly beast, its ancient founder according to a colorful folkloric tale of the city's origin.

After conquest by the Romans in 222 B.C., Milan became the major city of Cisalpine Gaul (Rome's Gallic lands south of the Alps). Under Emperor Augustus, it was second only to Rome itself. When the empire was split in two by Diocletian in the third century, Milan was declared the western emperor's residential and administrative capital, and rapidly proved a highly lucrative trading center between Italy and northern Europe.

Ambrose, Attila, and the Lombards

It was a provincial governor, Aurelius Ambrosius, sent from Rome's German colony of Trier in A.D. 374, who placed Milan firmly on the European map. His reputation for justice and personal incorruptibility so sparked popular approval that he became bishop of Milan, and was later canonized. Thanks to St. Ambrose's scrupulous leadership and resistance to less than scrupulous emperors, Milan became a pillar of the Christian church. To this day he holds firm the position of loving protector and patron saint of the city (see box on page 24).

Passing through the town in A.D. 452, Attila the Hun showed unsurprisingly little respect for Milan's spiritual values, leaving a characteristic combination of rape and pillage in his wake. The Goths followed suit in A.D. 538, burning the city to the ground.

Some 30 years later, the Milanese clergy and their flock were on the run again, seeking the protection of Greek-led Byzantine forces around Genoa against the latest wave of invaders, the Lombards. Originally from north Germany, the *Longobardi* or Long Beards launched their attack on Italy from the Danube valley. Passing quickly through deserted Milan, rough, tough King Alboin established his court at Pavia, which

Castello Sforzesco was rebuilt in its hulking present form during the 15th century.

he captured from the Byzantines in A.D. 572 after a three-year siege. He was murdered soon after, for forcing his wife to drink wine from the skull of her dead father.

To show the locals that they were not entirely barbarian, the Lombards set up courts of law, established an important school of jurisprudence at Pavia, and gradually abandoned their traditional system of vendetta. Their empire expanded through Italy as far down as the Duchy of Benevento, south of Naples.

The Lombards' most important king was one Liudprand (A.D. 712–744), who, acting in the best interests of a tactical alliance with native Roman Catholics against the outsider Byzantines, managed to persuade his fellow Lombards to give up the Arian heresy that they had brought with them from Germany.

By the time Charlemagne, king of the Franks, had conquered Lombardy, occupying Milan in A.D. 774, the people of Lombard and Roman stock had integrated to form what could be called the Italians.

The Middle Ages

In the ninth and tenth centuries, Milan bounced back. Yet again, it was the church that boosted the city's self-confidence. Under energetic Archbishop Ansperto da Biassono, the city walls were rebuilt. Trade soared, and the town soon showed off its prosperity by building two fine churches: Sant'Ambrogio and Sant'Eustorgio. In 1045, the city declared itself a commune with autonomous government, and was vying for supremacy with its Lombard rivals, Pavia, Cremona, Lodi, and Como.

Attracted by this new power and wealth, Frederick Barbarossa ("Redbeard") looked to annex Milan in his Holy Roman Empire. He smashed its city walls in 1162, but the

Milanese forces resisted and the war continued until 1183. In the meantime, a new Lombard League was formed (1167) under Milan's leadership to repel the foreign invader.

On 29 May 1176, the Lombard League's troops, bearing the ferocious name of *Compagnia della Morte* (Company of Death), defeated Frederick Barbarossa's German forces at Legnano, northwest of Milan. The victory was vital for the national consciousness since for the first time the battle cry was heard for "the freedom and honor of Italy."

Rise and Fall of the Visconti

The 13th century ushered in the era of the great dynastic families. The Ghibelline forces of Archbishop Ottone Visconti (supporting the emperor) routed the Torriani family representing the Guelph faction (supporting the pope) at Desio in 1277.

With a family name derived from a hereditary 11th-century title of viscount, the Archbishop Visconti was succeeded in 1295 by his great-nephew Matteo Visconti, who imposed a harsh, authoritarian rule over the commune and region. In gratitude for his military support, the German King Adolf of Nassau bestowed on him the title of Imperial Vicar of Lombardy. When this aroused the ire of Pope John XXII, Matteo (1250–1322) settled for *Signore* (Lord) of Milan. However, he did not escape excommunication on charges of heresy.

Milan prospered under the *signoria* (lordship) regardless. Its urban population of over 200,000 was the largest in Europe. Trade and industry—primarily textiles and metal-work—boomed, and Matteo controlled Milan and much of Lombardy with an army of mercenaries; there were no communal forces to resist and the merchants were all too busy making money to pay much attention to military matters.

Enriched by lands outside Milan and ensured of the support of the German emperor, the Visconti had broken free of dependence on the hitherto demanding local populace. At the time, theirs was the most aggressive state in the whole of 14th-century Italy.

The Visconti were also great patrons of the arts, and in their time began building Milan's magnificent cathedral, founded the great Certosa (charterhouse) di Pavia, and made the University of Pavia one of the finest and oldest in Europe. Gian Galeazzo Visconti (1351– 1402) was a disciple of the great poet Petrarch and ensured him a living by making him director of the Visconti library. He also developed a modern bureaucracy, conceiving state and government as a rationally planned "work of art." In 1395 he bought the title of Duke of Milan: through an alliance with Isabelle de Valois he was about to marry into the French royal family. Their daughter, Valentina, married the French king's brother.

The museum at Castello Sforzesco is rich in history.

Gian Galeazzo's strong hold on power led him to ignore his nominal allegiance to the German emperor. He hired and fired officials at will, imposed taxes and laws without consulting the

Milan would not be what it is today without the Church.

duchy's council, enforced mail-censorship, and controlled travel by introducing passports. The lands he expropriated at strategically sensitive points gave him almost total control of northern Italy, culminating in his seizure of Bologna in 1402. That same year, with his lordship established over Pisa, Siena and Perugia, he was poised to attack Florence when the plague providentially carried him off.

Visconti court etiquette had become highly refined and elaborate, distancing the rulers from the people. Arbitrary tax-gouging and law enforcement characterized an authority dependent entirely on autocratic rule. Thus, under Gian Galeazzo's mad heir, Giovanni Maria, the Visconti Empire quickly fell apart. By 1447, the dynasty had died out, though the female line passed through the Visconti to the Valois of France (notably Louis XII and François I, who were to stake claims to the duchy of Milan), as well as the Hapsburgs of Austria and Spain, and the Tudors of England.

Renaissance under the Sforzas

The day after the death of the last Visconti despot, Filippo Maria, Milan established an "Ambrosian Republic." Born more of an unresolved power struggle between rival factions of aristocrats than of a popular movement for democracy, it proved unable to control its hinterland and lasted only three years before yielding to Francesco Sforza in 1450. The *condottiere* (captain) asserted his claim to the duchy as the husband of an illegitimate Visconti daughter, Bianca Maria.

The powerful Sforza family had left their farms in Romagna, near Ravenna, to become mercenaries, offering their services in rapid succession to Ferrara, Naples, and Milan. When Francesco fell out with the Visconti, he joined the Medici of Florence and fought for them against Milan. Once installed as Duke of Milan, he actually formed an alliance with the Florentines against Venice and Naples.

Although no less despotic than the Visconti, the Sforza dynasty restored prosperity, particularly through expansion of the arms and silk industries, and brought a new artistic luster to the city. With his son, Galeazzo Maria Sforza, Francesco built the splendid Ospedale Maggiore and restored the formidable Castello Sforzesco. His other son, Ludovico, completed the bulk of the work on the cathedral and built a great tribune for the Church of

Detail of Como's Gothic-Renaissance cathedral.

Santa Maria delle Grazie and cloister for the Church of Sant'Ambrogio. He also expanded the network of canals for trade, and strengthened the city fortifications for defense against his enemies.

Deriving his nickname from his dark complexion and black hair, Ludovico il Moro ("the Moor") was politically less astute than his father but culturally the most brilliant of the Sforza dukes. He was a classical example of the Renaissance prince, ruthless in government, devious in diplomacy, and enlightened in his patronage of the arts. Among his protégés were the great architect Donato Bramante and Leonardo da Vinci. The glittering life of his court was famous throughout Europe.

Ludovico's lust for power pitted him against his mother in wresting the duchy from the rightful heir, his seven-year-old nephew, Gian Galeazzo, who had been "exiled" to a rival court in Pavia. Ludovico made and broke alliances with bewildering facility first with Naples against Venice, then with France against Naples, and finally with Venice against France. He remained, however, relatively loyal to his father-in-law, the powerful Duke of Ferrara, and to the German emperor, Maximilian I, who had formally confirmed his right to the title of duke.

His machinations did get the better of him when, fearing trouble from Gian Galeazzo's followers, he encouraged the invasion by Charles VIII of France to seize the throne of Naples in 1494. This fatal blunder marked the beginning of the end—not only for the duchy itself, but also for all of Italy's independent city states.

Alarmed by the success of Charles VIII's military campaign, Ludovico then backed a Venice-led league to drive the French back out of Italy the following year. He emerged from the campaign as a short-term winner, boasting that

Pope Alexander VI was now his chaplain, Emperor Maximilian his general, the Doge of Venice his chamberlain, and King Charles VIII his courier, but he had set in motion events that would prove his downfall. The historical novel *Duchess of Milan* details this period quite well; although a work of fiction, it includes actual excerpts from Leonardo da Vinci's correspondence.

The Biblioteca Ambrosiana is home to a great many historic masterpieces.

In 1499, King Louis XII, grandson on his mother's side of Valentina Visconti, declared the Sforzas to be usurpers and marched into Milan to claim the duchy for himself. Tired of paying heavy taxes to support the luxury of the Sforza court and the cost of the wars, the Milanese cheered their new master. Ludovico attempted a comeback in 1500, but was roundly defeated and spent the rest of his life in exile, in the gilded prison of a Loire Valley château.

Foreign Rule

For the next 360 years, Milan was a pawn in the rivalries of the main continental European powers—Spain, France,

Napoleon in Milan

Napoleon Bonaparte arrived in town to the cries of the Milanese: "Liberté, Egalité, Fraternité!" At a banquet in the Austrian archduke's palace, Napoleon assured the city's gentry: "You will be free. Milan will be the national capital. You will have 500 cannons and France's eternal friendship." That same night, from his quarters in the Palazzo Serbelloni he wrote home to Paris: "Don't worry, we'll get ten million francs from this place." Milan was then subjected to wholesale expropriations, plunder, taxes, and confiscation of precious art treasures from churches and private collections. Though most artworks were returned after the French defeat, some, like Titian's *Jesus Crowned with Thorns*, remain at the Louvre in Paris. It's only fair to add, however, that Napoleon also founded Milan's Fine Arts Academy and the Brera Museum, which now house much of the retrieved booty.

Among the many things for which Napoleon was blamed, one was the weather. The genteel Milanese ladies told their darling French novelist, Stendhal, that it had never been so cold until that wicked man dug a road through the Simplon Pass, opening a hole in the hitherto protective Alpine barrier.

and Austria. Unimaginative foreign rule and a series of plagues crippled Milan's economy. Among the few bright elements in two centuries of gloom were the forceful educational reforms of the city's archbishop, the enlightened Carlo Borromeo (1538–1584). (Conditions in this dark era of Milan's history are strikingly depicted in the celebrated novel of Alessandro Manzoni, *The Betrothed*, a must-read for every Italian high-school student.)

In 1706, during the War of Spanish Succession, the Hapsburgs installed Prince Eugene of Savoy as governor to enforce Austrian administration. The city was slow to emerge from stagnation, but under a more efficient government in the second half of the 18th century, the economy began to pick up. At this time, wealthy merchants built the first of the Neo-Classical buildings that dominate the urban landscape today. Cultural oppression, however, particularly in the form of censorship, drove writers and sociologists to form the *Società dei Pugni* (literally, Society of Fists), espousing the new ideas of the French Revolution.

After France's convincing defeat of the Austrians, Napoleon Bonaparte's soldiers were welcomed into the city as liberators in 1796. The Cisalpine Republic was proclaimed and the town flourished. In 1805, a grateful merchant bourgeoisie applauded the republic's transformation into the Kingdom of Italy, with Milan as capital, and Napoleon crowned himself king in the cathedral.

Despite France's controlling involvement, Milan became the dominant force in Italian trade. It developed a proud new image, mod-

Leonardo da Vinci presides over the Piazza della Scala.

ernized by Napoleonic reforms in administration, scientific academies, and French-style high-school education for both boys and girls.

However, progress was halted by the collapse of the Napoleonic Empire and the return of conquering Austrian forces in 1814. Milan remained under Hapsburg rule for another 50 years. Though eager to exploit the city's prosperity, the regime remained as oppressive as ever. This time, imbued with a new self-assurance from contact with the French, the Milanese were quick to resist. Poised at the forefront of the *Risorgimento* movement for national unity, the Milanese staged an important revolt in March 1848. They liberated the city for a glorious but brief four months before being brutally crushed by the Austrian army. Several streets and squares all over Lombardy are named after those significant five days, *Cinque Giornate*.

Following victory over the Austrians at Marengo in 1859, Vittorio Emanuele, the first king of independent Italy, entered the city with his French ally Napoleon III. They came in through the triumphal arch (now known as Arco della Pace), which had been designed for the French emperor's uncle 50 years earlier.

The Stazione Centrale, a study in Fascist design.

Leonardo the Plumber

As Renaissance men went, few could match the universal talents of Tuscany-born Leonardo da Vinci (1452–1519), whose skills covered everything from mathematics and botany to aviation, sculpture, architecture and, on the side, a little painting. In 1482, when he left Florence for the court of Ludovico Sforza in Milan, his calling card was that of a musician. In his application for work, Leonardo himself listed his talents as a builder of cannons and fortifications, and master of piping for water and heat. He added as an afterthought: "I can carry out sculpture in marble, bronze or clay, and... in painting I can do as well as any man."

During his 18 prolific years in Milan, Leonardo spent most of his time as a glorified odd-job man around the Castello Sforzesco. In spare moments, he painted the ***Last Supper*** (1495–1497) at the church of Santa Maria delle Grazie (see page 41), *Portrait of a Musician* at the Ambrosiana Library, the *Virgin of the Rocks* (c. 1483–1485) now hanging in the Louvre, and the *Litta Madonna*, now in the Hermitage in St. Petersburg. He also knocked off quick court commissions to portray Ludovico's mistresses, notably Cecilia Gallerani, which is now in Cracow.

Thereafter, Milan remained in the vanguard of Italy's belated but dynamic industrial and commercial revolution. In the boom years, metal, chemical, and textile factories sprang up around the city's periphery, while publishing companies, banks, and the stock exchange dominated the center. In the bold iron-and-glass roof of the Neo-Renaissance Galleria Vittorio Emanuele shopping arcade (see page 33), progress was given an architectural symbol. Leaving the political tangle to Rome, Milan was content with its role as the country's business capital, a division of power and attitude that survives to this day.

Freedom and Fascism

At the turn of the 20th century, the city was a hotbed of radical political movement. It had elected its first Socialist mayor in the 1890s, and the Milanese newspapers, book publishers, and university had assembled Italy's most progressive minds.

In 1898, with the conservatives back in power, food riots protesting high wheat prices (essential for the daily pasta) led to the closure of the university and the presence of the army to enforce control. Its cannons left 100 dead and 600 wounded, including monks fired on by mistake

Self-Made Saint

Aurelius Ambrosius (c. A.D. 334 or 340–397) was a no-nonsense bishop. Born of Christian parents but with no religious training, this Roman civil servant responded to his unexpected appointment by taking a crash course in theology. He was willing to "render unto Caesar" but not to let Caesar ride roughshod over his ideas of God. After his studies convinced him of the evil of Arianism (a then-popular belief denying that Jesus was consubstantial with God), he refused the demand of Emperor Valentinian to hand over one of Milan's churches to the Arians. Emperor Theodosius I conceded, but when he then massacred thousands of rebels in Thessalonica, Ambrosius not only excommunicated him but also made him come to Milan and prostrate himself in penance at the cathedral. Of Theodosius, Ambrosius said: "The emperor is within the church; he is not above it."

when a crowd of beggars was waiting for soup outside their monastery.

It was in Milan in 1919 that Benito Mussolini founded his *Fasci Italiani di Combattimento* or Italian Combat League, simply known to history as the Fascists. In a hall lent by a circle of local merchants and industrialists, the ex-Socialist newspaperman assembled 60 anti-parliamentarians stirred by the ultranationalist sentiments of World War I. They started their campaign by drowning out Democratic speeches held at La Scala, but quickly moved to more characteristic activities like burning the Milan headquarters of the Socialist newspaper, *Avanti!* After skillfully fanning the flames of the movement across the country, *il Duce* returned to Milan in 1922 to mastermind the March on Rome of 26,000 Blackshirts. So ended Italy's brief experience of democracy.

Fascism was an ambivalent and ultimately horrific experience for Milan. Archbishop Ildefonso Schuster and Monsignor Agostino Gemelli, rector of the Catholic University, proved enthusiastic supporters of the cause, but the town was also a principal center of the anti-Fascist group *Giustizia e Libertà*.

In World War II, the city suffered 15 bombardments, the heaviest of which occurred in 1943. The following year, Milan staged the nation's first general strike in protest against the war, leading to hundreds of workers being deported to German concentration camps. Fascist militia hanged 15 partisans on the Piazza Loreto where, just nine months later, Fascist leaders themselves were executed by partisan firing squads, and the corpses of Mussolini and his mistress Clara Petacci were strung up just a stone's throw from the *Stazione Centrale,* his own monument standing in Milan.

Cold Shoulder

In January 1857, the crowds turned out for the Milan visit of Austria's Emperor Franz-Josef with his new bride Elizabeth ("Sissi") and greeted them not with violent demonstrations but with devastating silence. Fearing a boycott of the imperial couple's night at the opera at La Scala, the Austrians prepared to fill the boxes with their own people in borrowed eveningwear. When obliged to say whether they would be using their subscription tickets, Milan's great families replied in the affirmative and then sent their servants instead.

After 1945, Milan recovered quickly, taking a leading role in the country's economic miracle (but also in the crisis of confidence caused by the nationwide bribery scandals of the 1990s). It has long boasted to have the lion's share of Italy's major banks, its stock market, and its trade fairs. And Milan's suburbs are home to a range of heavy industries. In 1993, the discredited Socialist party, which for years had made the mayoralty its domain, gave way to the right-wing party of the Lombard League. In 1994, this was repeated in national elections, when the League, with Milan's TV-mogul Silvio Berlusconi's *Forza Italia* and the far right National Alliance Party (*Alleanza Nazionale*), the former neo-Fascist MSI party, gained the victory. (Berlusconi, as Prime Minister, would go on to form Italy's 59th postwar government in June 2001.) Constantly changing politics are harder to keep up with than the rise and fall of the catwalk's hemlines. Throughout it all, the Milanese continue to succeed at what they do best: hard work, and hard play.

Historical Landmarks

600 B.C.	First settlement established by the Gauls.
222 B.C.	Conquest by the Romans.
Third cen. A.D.	Mediolanum is capital of Western Roman Empire.
452	Attila the Hun plunders the city.
568	The Lombards invade, make Pavia their capital.
774	Charlemagne enters Milan, ending Lombard rule.
1045	Milan constitutes itself an autonomous commune.
1176	Lombard League defeats Barbarossa at Legnano.
1277	Ghibelline Visconti defeat Guelf Torriani at Desio Milan is Europe's largest city (pop. 200,000).
1351–1402	Gian Galeazzo Visconti starts Milan's Cathedral.
1447–1450	Ambrosian Republic.
1450–1466	Francesco Sforza becomes Duke of Milan.
1466–1499	Ludovico Sforza sponsors Leonardo da Vinci.
1499	King Louis XII of France seizes Duchy of Milan.
1535	Control seized by Charles V.
1540–1706	Spanish rule.
1706	Prince Eugene of Savoy installs Austrian regime.
1796–1814	Napoleon makes Milan capital of his Cisalpine Republic, then of the Kingdom of Italy (1805).
1814–1859	Rise of Risorgimento independence movement.
1859	Milan heads Italy's industrial revolution.
1890s	First Socialist city government is elected.
1919	Mussolini founds the Fascist movement in Milan.
1939–1945	World War II; Milan suffers heavy bombardment.
1960s–1980s	Milan helps to revive Italian economy.
1993	Right-wing Lombard League mayor elected.
1994	Berlusconi's "Forza Italia" wins general election.
1995	Maurizio Gucci murdered in Milan.
1997	Gianni Versace murdered in Florida.
2001	La Scala Opera House closes for renovation.

WHERE TO GO

The region of Lombardy, covering Milan and the lakes, can be divided into five areas for sightseeing. The city of Milan itself; excursions to the nearby towns of Monza, Pavia, and Bergamo (all possible day trips from Milan); and the three lakes from west to east: Maggiore, Como, and Garda.

MILAN

Even though Milan is one of the largest Italian cities, you can get a good feel for its most interesting attractions in just a day or two. Start in the area around the Duomo (cathedral) and La Scala Opera House, taking time to visit the shopping district around Via Montenapoleone. Then, head for the Castello Sforzesco and its park before going on to Leonardo's *Last Supper,* his science museum, and Sant'Ambrogio Church.

Keep a few hours for the Brera Museum and the nearby galleries, and then take your pick from the other museums and churches in the city. Those with more time might choose to explore Milan's outskirts, and between sights can relax on a café terrace in the artists' neighborhood of the Navigli canal district to watch the parade of fashionable Milanese while you sip an *aperitivo* and contemplate the many aspects of Italy's most vibrant metropolis.

Most of Milan's major sights are within comfortable walking distance. The tram-and-bus system can be tricky, but the well-organized subway *(Metropolitana)* is straightforward and self-explanatory.

Piazza del Duomo

Few of the world's great cities have such an obvious focus for beginning a visit as the **Piazza del Duomo**. Rounding the corner of the piazza, your breath is taken away by the sheer grandness and flamboyant detail of the cathedral commanding the square. Designed by Giuseppe Mengoni, architect of the adjoining Galleria Vittorio Emanuele, the square and arcades around the cathedral have for centuries provided a natural meeting place for both the Milanese and their pigeons.

As both geographical and psychological center of Milan, there is nonstop bustle during the day. Have a seat on the steps in front of the Duomo and catch a glamorous model walking by, a smartly dressed banker on his lunch break, a student sketching, or an Italian television diva waiting to meet her agent. As the sun sets, you will see the bars under the Portici Settentrionali filling up with snappily dressed men and women having a drink and munching on bar snacks before their dinner appointments during the magical moment of the late-afternoon *passeggiata*.

The Cathedral

Milan's **Duomo** is the most grandiose of Italy's Gothic cathedrals. Begun in 1386 on the site of an earlier church (Santa Maria Maggiore), it took nearly six centuries to complete. The exterior of the cathe-

The exquisite Duomo looms over the lively piazza and its pigeon residents.

dral was completely restored in time for the 2000 Jubilee, and the colour of the cathedral's white marble – taken from the nearby lake district – is resplendent even on a typically grey Milan day. Look up to the highest pinnacle crowned by the golden statue of the *Madonnina* to whom the city's anthem is dedicated.

Duke Gian Galeazzo Visconti founded the church as a votive offering to God in his plight for a male heir. His plan worked, but his architectural demands proved too much for the local masons from nearby Lake Como, and French, Flemish, and German architects had to be called in to help. The major Italian contribution was by Pellegrino Tibaldi, who worked in

The main altar inside the Duomo—one of many architectural wonders within this grandiose cathedral.

the 16th century mainly on the interior, under the direction of revered Archbishop Carlo Borromeo (see page 20). The main spire was erected in the 18th century, the façade was completed under Napoleon in 1813, and work on other spires and exterior sculpture continued right up until the 20th century.

To best take in the bristling silhouette of marble pinnacles and statues and the awesomely flamboyant façade, stand on the south side of the cathedral in the courtyard of the Palazzo Reale. Despite the quite visible northern European influence, the Duomo presents a much wider and more "horizontal" appearance than the majority of Gothic cathedrals in France and Germany.

Inside, the vast and noble space of the nave and four aisles shows more clearly the church's northern inspiration, particularly in the 52 soaring columns and the decoration of **stained-glass windows**, dating from the 15th century to the present day. The most precious stained glass, tracing the story of St. John the Evangelist, is to be seen in the south aisle (to the right). A 13th-century Visconti archbishop lies in the red marble sarcophagus mounted on pillars. In the right-hand transept, notice the matter-of-fact treatment of an horrific martyrdom in Marco d'Agrate's 1562 **statue of St Bartholomew**: flayed alive, he is carrying his own skin.

A door to the right of the high altar leads down to the cathedral's **crypt**, where you can see an ancient reliquary and ivory carvings from the fourth and fifth centuries. The remains of Archbishop Carlo Borromeo are displayed here, draped in opulent finery.

Back in the north transept you'll find the monumental 14th-century **Trivulzio Candelabrum**, with its seven branches of bronze.

Make some time for every traveler's favorite Milanese experience: a spectacular walk out on the **roof** – in warmer weather, the profane can cultivate a suntan here. The elevator entrance (clearly marked outside the Duomo) is in the south (right) transept. Wander high above the city, beneath the flying buttresses and around the statues (2,245 in all) and pinnacles (135), and climb up to the roof ridge for an unbeatable view of Milan—with the not-too-distant Alps on those rare days that pollution does not veil their proximity. Make your way over to the apse at the rear of the roof for a close-up of the three magnificent Gothic windows. The intricately carved, white-marble tracery and other roof sculpture are unique in Italian architecture.

In the cathedral's west façade, a separate entrance leads to the octagonal, fourth-century **baptistery**, where St Ambrose baptized St Augustine in 387.

Palazzo Reale

South of the cathedral (adjoining the main Tourist Office at the corner of Via Marconi), the **Palazzo Reale**, former residence of Milan's Spanish and Austrian governors, houses today the **Museo del Duomo** (Cathedral Museum) in its south wing. It displays impressive Gothic sculpture from the cathedral exterior, casts of the countless statues gracing the Duomo's rooftop, a likeness of Gian Galeazzo Visconti, handsome 15th-century stained glass, Tintoretto's *Child Jesus with the Rabbis,* and a good model of the Duomo as it was conceived in 1519.

On the palazzo's upper floor (accessible from the main courtyard) is the **Civico Museo di Arte Contemporaneo** (better known as CIMAC, Museum of Modern Art) with paintings by Giorgio Chirico, Giorgio Morandi, Filippo de Pisis, and the Futurists Carlo Carrà, Umberto Boccioni, Giacomo Balla, and Gino Severini. There is also sculpture by Lucio Fontana and Arturo Martini.

A quick walk farther south takes you over to the massive Renaissance **Ospedale Maggiore**, the main building of the University of Milan since 1958. Founded as a hospital by the Milanese Duke Francesco Sforza in 1456, the terracotta design of the right wing is by Antonio Filarete, architect of the Castello Sforzesco. Take a look inside at the grand central cloisters.

Piazza Mercanti

From the northwest corner of the Piazza del Duomo, take Via Mercanti, leading to the only medieval area in the city to have survived the devastating bombs of World War II and the wrecking ball of zealous post-war building developers.

Before the cathedral was built, Piazza Mercanti was the center of city life, with the seat of communal government, the Romanesque **Palazzo della Ragione** (1233), on its south side. It was the birthplace of the Milanese "stock market," as all trade and bartering of goods was carried out under its porticoes. Notice the relief of a *scrofa semilanuta*, a wild boar-like animal claimed to be the city's namesake. Also note the fine equestrian relief of the 13th-century chief magistrate Oldrado da Tressano, by the Roman sculptor Benedetto Antelami, above one of the pillars. The elegant upper story was added in 1770. On the opposite side of the piazza, in black-and-white marble, is the Gothic **Loggia degli Osii** (c. 1316) and the Baroque **Palazzo delle Scuole Palatine**.

Galleria Vittorio Emanuele II

Back on the north side of the Piazza del Duomo, through a triumphal arch, the massive, cross-shaped shopping gallery is a grand steel-and-glass vaulted monument to the expansive commercial spirit of the 19th century.

Inside the glorious Galleria Vittorio Emanuele II.

For cafés such as the famous Zucca's, restaurants, boutiques, bookshops, and travel agencies, architect Giuseppe Mengoni provided an appropriate Neo-Renaissance décor delightfully cool in summer, but a little drafty in winter. Sadly, a couple of days before the gallery's inauguration in 1878, Mengoni fell to his death from the roof. Sadder still, American fast-food chains have elbowed in between the beautiful antique traditional cafés. If you feel like you need a little luck, take a spin on the "balls of the bull" depicted on the western part of the intricate central mosaic flooring. Tradition dictates that anyone who spins on their left heel 360 degrees in one go will have good luck for their duration of their stay in Milan.

☛ La Scala Opera House

The Galleria offers a convenient passage from the Duomo to another holy of holies, La Scala—that 18th-century temple of musical drama, and probably the world's most celebrated opera house. (Its name is derived from the church it replaced, Santa Maria della Scala, which in turn was named after Regina della Scala, wife of a Visconti duke.) In contrast to the theatre's lush interior – there are 2,800 in 260 boxes, four balconies, and the "gods" (see page 85 for more details) – the façade is sober, even austere, perhaps because architect Giuseppe Piermarini did not want to compete with the brilliance of the carriages pulling up under his portico.

The opera house closed for extensive restoration in late 2001 and is due to remain under wraps until the end of 2004. During La Scala's closure, opera is being performed at the newly built, ultra-contemporary 2,400-seat **Teatro degli Arcimboldi**, situated in zona Bicocca, an old industrial area northwest of Milan's Stazione Centrale.

Opera fans may wish to take a detour to the **Museo Teatrale** (Theater Museum), formerly housed in a building

The Museo Teatrale linked to La Scala holds such fascinating relics of history as this manuscript by Verdi.

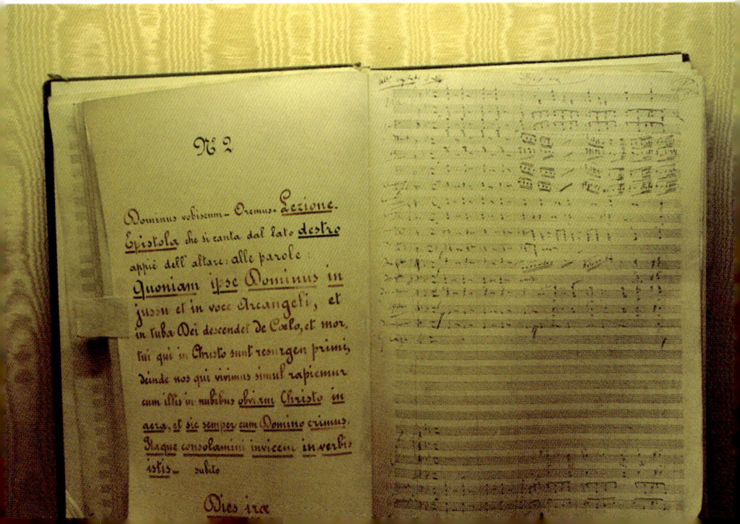

Puppets beckon visitors at Milan's Museo Teatrale.

adjacent to La Scala but relocated in 2002 to Palazzo Busca (Corso Magenta 71, tel: 02 469 12 49, open daily 9am–6pm, last admission 5.15pm). The museum traces the fascinating history of opera and theatre in the city, with memorabilia of composers including Verdi, Bellini, and Donizetti on show.

Back in Piazza La Scala, just across the square from the Opera House, is Milan's handsome, 16th-century town hall, **Palazzo Marino**. In the centre of the square is a restored yet still unprepossessing 19th-century monument to Leonardo da Vinci and his pupils.

Via Montenapoleone

Only a few select shopping districts in the world achieve the status of monuments, and right up there with London's Bond Street, New York's Fifth Avenue, Los Angeles's Rodeo Drive, and Paris's Rue du Faubourg St. Honoré, is Milan's last word in shopping: the **Via Montenapoleone** (referred to in some guidebooks as "Montenapo," although locals rarely use the nickname).

Reached north of the Piazza La Scala along Via Alessandro Manzoni, the neighbourhood in which it lies is a veritable living exhibition of Milan's exquisite sense of modern and classical design at its very polished. Fashion, jewellery, furniture, and luxurious household accessories are all on dazzling show along Via Montenapoleone and **Via della Spiga**. Countless shops of equal pedigree have long spilled over onto the web of narrow streets between them. Stop in at the historical Bar **Cova**, famous for allegedly having invented the sacher torte. Ladies who shop don't miss an afternoon respite here: ask for their renowned house cocktail, the *aperitivo Cova*.

This is Italy's finest window shopping, amidst a setting of elegant 18th-century palazzi housing deluxe boutiques with theatrical window displays that are works of art in themselves. Beyond the predominantly warm, yellow tones of the façades, explore the beautiful inner courtyards, which are wonderful havens of peace away from the city bustle. Nearby, everybody rushes on **Via Bagutta**, with its famous

A statue of the great artist Leonardo da Vinci, on Piazza La Scala.

bistro that shares the same name (see page 134), and along **Via Sant'Andrea**, **Via Gesù**, **Via Verri**, **Via Santo Spirito,** and **Via Borgospessi**.

Castello Sforzesco

A fortress with a checkered past, Castello Sforzesco is now an art museum.

The huge brick fortress northwest of the city center (Metro: Cairoli) was rebuilt in its present form in the 15th century by Duke Francesco Sforza. It stands on the site of a Visconti castle destroyed by citizens of the short-lived Ambrosian Republic (see page 16). Used by the Spanish as a stronghold and by the Austrians as a refuge from the Italian uprising of 1848, it was converted to an art museum in the 1950s.

The four-square structure surrounds an interior courtyard, **Piazza d'Armi**, where fine summer concerts are held among the architectural fragments assembled here from other city monuments.

The main tower follows a Renaissance design by Florentine architect Antonio Filarete, and is therefore named after him. Roman master Donato Bramante contributed part of the other work, with some interior décor—

and plumbing (see page 23)—by Renaissance man Leonardo da Vinci.

The palace apartments were in the **Corte Ducale** over to the right, now the entrance to the **Musei del Castello** (Castle Museums), which has a pioneering modern art display in an antique setting.

The *Arte Antica* collections of ancient and medieval art are devoted mostly to sculpture, notably including a Roman sarcophagus and some interesting statuary from Byzantine, Romanesque, and Gothic churches. Notice, too, the Gothic tombs of Bernabò Visconti, one of the more sadistically violent members of the Visconti clan, and his wife Regina della Scala, whose name survives in the opera house (see page 34).

The **frescoes** in room 8, *Sala delle Asse,* in the north-east corner of the castle were done by Leonardo da Vinci but have since been badly damaged by unfortunate over-restoration.

Room 15, *Sala degli Scarlioni,* is reserved for the Castello Sforzesco's unfinished but still marvelous treasure, Michelangelo's

Stained glass, among the many treasures you'll find at Castello Sforzesco.

☛ moving ***Rondanini Pietà***. Named after its original home in the Palazzo Rondanini in Rome, it is a poignant, vertical treatment of Mary struggling to hold up the body of her crucified son.

Michelangelo worked on the piece on and off for nine years and was still chiselling away at it just six days before his death in 1564. There is a strange pathos in the great Renaissance master returning to Gothic forms for his last work in his 89th year. Nearby is a bronze bust of Michelangelo by his sculptor friend, Daniele da Volterra.

On the other side of the Corte Ducale, the **Pinacoteca** is home to important paintings by masters including Giovanni Bellini, Mantegna, Correggio, Titian, Lorenzo Lotto, Tintoretto, and Tiepolo. Local Lombard artists Foppa and Bergognone, and Leonardo's disciples Boltraffio and Sodoma are also represented.

Over in the **Rocchetta**, once the Palazzo's guards' room and where the inhabitants of the castle hid in times of seige, are fine Egyptian and archaeological collections, as well as ceramics and furniture.

Parco Sempione

At the back of the Castello, the Sforza family's old hunting grounds were transformed at the end of the 19th century into delightful public gardens carefully laid out as an English landscaped park.

The pace here is leisurely, away from the brisk bustle of the center, but unfortunately it does show evidence of city life. In the right-hand corner of Parco Sempione is an **aquarium** of exotic tropical fish. Over on the left side of the park is the **Palazzo del Arte**, a thoroughly modern exhibition hall, most noted for the world-famous *Triennale* show of decorative arts.

A fine **equestrian statue** by Francesco Barzagli in the middle of the park commemorates Napoleon III's passage through the Neo-Classical **Arco della Pace** at the far end of the park, after the Italian-French victory over the Austrians in 1859 (see page 22). The triumphal arch, completed in 1838 is the starting point of the Corso Sempione, the Simplon Road that Napoleon Bonaparte ordered to be built through the Alps, whose presence reputedly influenced local climatic conditions (see page 20).

Leonardo's Milan

Leonardo spent 18 years in the service of Duke Ludovico Sforza (see page 17), and several monuments testify to the artist's presence in the city.

From the west side of the Castello Sforzesco (Metro: Cadorna), you are within easy walking distance of two monuments which demonstrate the different sides of Leonardo da Vinci's genius. His acclaimed artistic masterpiece, the *Last Supper,* is housed in the old Dominican monastery (see page 42), and his scientific inventions in the **Museo della Scienza e della Tecnica** (Science and Technology Museum; see page 43). The church of Sant'Ambrogio, Milan's most venerated place of worship, is conveniently nearby.

Even without Leonardo da Vinci's painting in the adjoining building, the church of **Santa Maria delle Grazie** (on Piazza Santa Maria della Grazia) is a jewel of Renaissance architecture. A restoration of the church's interior has been underway since 2001. Adding to an earlier Gothic design, in 1492 Donato Bramante—Pope Julius II's chief architect in Rome—fashioned a magnificent red-brick and white-stone **chancel** (*tribuna*) towering over the rear of the church. The graceful lines of the rectangular choir and 16-sided cupola

Michelangelo's poignant "Rondanini Pietà," dramatically lit inside the Castello Sforzesco museum.

are best viewed from the little **cloister** that Bramante built on the north side. Once inside the church, which was originally conceived as the Sforza family's burial place (the tombs of Ludovico il Moro and his wife Beatrice are to be restored to their rightful place here), stand in the choir to appreciate the full majesty of the chancel's dome. Notice, too, the exquisite inlaid wood and carving of the prayer stalls in the apse.

After being painstakingly restored recently Leonardo da Vinci's ***Last Supper*** (*Cenacolo*, 1498) is on view once again on one of the walls of the little Dominican refectory to the left of the church. Despite centuries of deterioration and a number of clumsy restorations since it was completed, the painting still carries enormous psychological impact. In the moment Leonardo has chosen to capture in his painting, we see the trauma of each of the disciples following Jesus' declaration: "One of you will betray me."

Almost as awe-inspiring as the painting itself is the inch-by-inch recovery of the fragmentary but still powerful traces of the "real Leonardo." The recent restoration reveals, for example, that Philip (third to the right, leaning over towards Jesus) has an expression of acute grief, not the simpering pathos left by past "restorers" who presumed to improve on the original. Since this is one of Milan's principal sights, booking at least three days in advance is essential (tel. 02/89421146).

On the wall opposite, the superb condition of Donato da Montorfano's *Crucifixion* (dating from 1495) shows how much better preserved Leonardo's work would have been if he had only accepted the constraints of fresco (see box. page 23) but the *Last Supper* would then perhaps have been less emotionally inspired as a painting.

For the other, equally fascinating aspect of Leonardo's talents visit the **Museo della Scienza e della Tecnica** (Science and Technology Museum) in the nearby Via San Vittore. Among the rooms devoted to scientific history, one gallery is reserved for **Leonardo's inventions**. They are displayed as models, constructed from details in his notebooks. You will see his aircraft, a machine for making screws, a revolving bridge, an hydraulic timber-cutter, some machine-tools, and a system of map-making by aerial views long before any aircraft, even his own, had become operational.

The Basilico of Sant'Ambrogio

At the eastern end of Via San Vittore, beyond a noble atrium, Milan's most revered sanctuary, dedicated to the city's patron saint, was built between the ninth and 12th centuries.

Leonardo da Vinci's iconographic "Last Supper", inside the church of Santa Maria delle Grazie.

It stands on the site of a church built in A.D. 386, founded by Aurelius Ambrosius, first Bishop of Milan, along with Peter, Paul, and Jerome (see page 11). Its position, next to the Catholic University, honors the scholarship of the man who left a revered personal legacy of hymns and philosophical homilies, so convincingly sweet with his words that his name gave us the word "ambrosia".

The sober, five-bayed façade is characteristic Lombard Romanesque, flanked by a ninth-century campanile on the right and a taller 12th-century tower to the left, and topped by a modern loggia.

In the interior, left of the handsome rib-vaulted nave, notice the 11th-century **pulpit** standing over a Christian sarcophagus of the Roman era. In the north (left) aisle are Bergognone's painting of *Jesus the Redeemer* and Bernardino

Luini's *Madonna*, in the south (right) aisle, frescoes by Tiepolo. The **high altar**, covered in gold and silver and richly embedded with precious stones, stands beneath a ninth-century canopy carved with Byzantine-Romanesque reliefs.

The remains of St. Ambrose himself are buried in the **crypt** beneath the presbytery at the far-east end of the church. The nearby church **museum** displaying early Christian mosaics, medieval sculpture, and frescoes by Bergognone and Luini is closed indefinitely for restoration.

The Brera

Just a short walk east of the Castello Sforzesco, the handsome 17th-century palace of the Jesuits today houses the **Pinacoteca di Brera**, one of Italy's foremost art museums, with an unrivalled collection of northern-Italian painting.

Visitors admire one of the many masterpieces housed in the Pinacoteca di Brera, one of Italy's foremost museums.

Bellini's "Madonna and Child" is one of the sublime highlights of the Pinacoteca di Brera's collection.

In its fine arcaded courtyard, notice a bronze statue of Napoleon—a remarkable, rare example of the emperor without clothes. (The marble original is at Apsley House, London.) Homage is paid here to Napoleon Bonaparte for turning the Brera into a national gallery with the art he confiscated from the Church and recalcitrant nobles. Most of what he expropriated in Italy for the Louvre in Paris ended up back in Milan at the Brera after Waterloo.

Among the highlights are: paintings by Giovanni Bellini of the *Madonna and Child* and an exquisitely personal *Pietà*; two Titian portraits, *Antonio Porcia* and *St. Jerome*; Veronese's *Jesus in the Garden*; Tintoretto's dramatic *Discovery of St. Mark's Body*; and an impressive *Jesus at the Column* by the many-talented Donato Bramante.

Mantegna's works include a touching *Madonna,* but his masterpiece here is the *Dead Jesus,* which achieves a gripping emotional effect. Piero della Francesca's celebrated *Montefeltro Altarpiece* (1474) was his last work.

The ethereal beauty of Correggio's *Nativity* and *Adoration of the Magi* and Raphael's stately *Betrothal of the Madonna* contrast with the earthier inspiration of Caravaggio's *Supper at Emmaus*.

Lombard masters include Bergognone, Boltraffio, Foppa, and Luini, while the non-Italian artists represented include El Greco, Rubens, Van Dyck, and Rembrandt. The modern collection has notable works by Modigliani, Boccioni, de Chirico, Carrà, and de Pisis.

The Artists' Quarter

Immediately west of the Pinacoteca di Brera, artists and antiques dealers alike vie for the high-rent galleries and shops along **Via Fiori Chiari** and **Via Madonnini** and around the **Piazza Formentini**.

Resisting the urge to lug back home that oversized hand-carved picture frame displayed at the popular **flea market** that takes place on the third Sunday of each month does not mean you cannot spend a few pleasant hours perusing the venders' wares. Enjoy lunch in any of Brera's trendy cafés or restaurants before, during, or after.

Other Museums and Churches

Museo Poldi-Pezzoli

This museum, on Via Alessandro Manzoni 12, has the precious charm of a formerly private collection, which not only contains a number of splendid paintings, but also antique watches, sundials, Murano glass and fine 16th-century Persian carpets, as well as soldiers' chain mail and face armour.

Among its prodigious collection of painted masterpieces are a Giovanni Bellini *Pietà*, Piero della Francesca's *San Nicola da Toledano*, Mantegna's *Madonna and Child*, a Botticelli *Madonna*, Antonio Pollaiuoli's lovely *Portrait of a Young Woman* and important works by Palma il Vecchio, Filippo Lippi, Perugino, Lorenzo Lotto, Tiepolo, and the Lombard masters.

Biblioteca Ambrosiana

Situated on Piazza Pio XI, 2, the Ambrosiana has recently undergone a full renovation. Its great library was originally housed in the 17th-century palace of the illustrious Cardinal Federigo Borromeo (nephew of the great Italian churchman, Archbishop Carlo Borromeo; see page 20). Among its precious manuscripts are Leonardo da Vinci's drawings, which illustrate his scientific and artistic theories.

The Ambrosiana's superb art gallery has as one of its

There's plenty to absorb in the Biblioteca Ambrosiana.

most precious treasures Leonardo's luminous *Portrait of a Musician* (1485), unfinished but the best preserved of the master's few surviving works. You can see his pervasive influence on Milanese artists in the decorative paintings of Bernardino Luini and in the *Portrait of a Young Woman* by artist Ambrogio de Predis.

There's nothing sweet about Caravaggio's *Bowl of Fruit* —the worm is already in the apple and the leaves are withering. Titian is also well represented at the Ambrosiana, notably with an imposing *Adoration of the Magi.*

One of the most fascinating exhibits, however, particularly for those who know Raphael's great *School of Athens* fresco in the Vatican, are the great Renaissance master's so-called "cartoons"—his preparatory drawings for the piece.

Museo Archeologico

Situated on Corso Magenta 15, the archaeological museum harbors a collection of Greek, Etruscan, and Roman antiquities—namely sculpture, sarcophagi, and ceramics in the former 16th-century **Monastero Maggiore** (entrance is through the cloisters). In the monastery's lay chapel there are several frescoes by artist Bernardino Luini.

Museo di Milano

The municipal museum, on Via Sant'Andrea 6, in the 18th-century Palazzo Morando, traces the city's history through a series of paintings, drawings and prints. The specific history of Italy's independence movement in the 19th century is recounted in the **Museo del Risorgimento** on Via Borgonuovo 23, housing a collection of works from the middle of the seventh century up to 1870. Included is an important collection of flags, decorations of the crowning of Napoleon I as king of Italy as well as some works by Giuseppe Mazzini.

San Satiro Church

Standing off the busy Via Torino near the Ambrosiana library (see page 48), San Satiro is a major work of Renaissance modelling (1478) by Donato Bramante. Walk around to Via Falcone to view its fine exterior, the 11th-century campanile, and newly restored **Cappella della Pietà**. The handsome interior has a characteristic Milanese décor of terracotta. A Greek cross space is created by an optical illusion. Over the high altar is a 13th-century *Madonna and Child* fresco. Notice the elegant, octagonal Renaissance **baptistery** off the south (right) aisle.

Church of San Lorenzo Maggiore

San Lorenzo Maggiore is situated south of the city center, near the ancient **Porta Ticinese**, and the 16 Corinthian columns from a temple portico, which together comprise Milan's only substantial Roman remains. With its late 19th-century façade, the Romanesque church stands on the site of an early Christian church founded in the fourth century. To mark that era is a striking bronze statue (recast) of Emperor Constantine.

San Lorenzo's outstanding feature, on the south (right) side, is the octagonal **Chapel of Sant'Aquilino** built in the fourth century as an imperial mausoleum. Inside are fifth-century mosaics of Jesus, the Apostles, and Elijah, an early Christian sarcophagus, and Roman architectural fragments.

☛ *Sant'Eustorgio Church*

A park, **Parco delle Basiliche**, stretches south of San Lorenzo Maggiore down to the medieval church **Sant' Eustorgio**, started in the 11th century and harmoniously expanded over the next 400 years. Notable additions are the fine **campanile** and the **Capella Portinari**, a jewel of

Renaissance architecture. The chapel, visited separately (donation requested), is dedicated to St. Peter the Martyr, a 13th-century inquisitor murdered by one of his victims and honored here with masterly frescoes (1468) by Vincenzo Foppa.

Just as impressive is the St. Peter's **tomb** sculpted by Giovanni di Balduccio in 1339. Off the south (right) transept, the huge Roman sarcophagus in the **Chapel of the Magi** held the relics of the three kings until 1164, when they moved to Cologne, Germany.

Santa Maria Maggiore, Milan's most venerable edifice.

Church of Santa Maria presso San Celso

Santa Maria presso San Celso, on Corso Italia, is a Romanesque church with a tenth-century bell-tower. Visit it on a bright day, in order to view Paris Bordone's beautiful *Holy Family with St. Jerome* and 14th-century frescoes in the south (right) aisle, as well as the handsome inlaid-wood **choir stalls**. In the north (left) aisle is Bergognone's *Jesus in the Stable*.

Away from the City Center

So many of Milan's churches, monuments, and museums are concentrated in and around the Duomo that few visitors venture any further. The following are some of the sights worth exploring outside the city center for those with extra time.

Navigli Canal District

Once a modest but colorful working-class neighborhood on the south side of town, the *Navigli* district has become a regentrified neighborhood, hugely popular for its prodigious bars, trendy bistros, open-air cafés, boutiques, galleries and artists' studios.

Two canals start out from the **Darsena basin** near the sprawling Piazza XXIV Maggio (where a pompous arch celebrates Napoleon III's victory over the Austrians at Marengo; see page 22). The **Naviglio Grande** runs west out to Abbiategrasso, and the **Naviglio Pavese** south to Pavia. They were originally dug in the Middle Ages to bring agricultural products into the city from the fertile plains, and by the 17th century they also served the gentry as waterways to their country villas.

From May to mid-September guided cruises are offered on the Naviglio Grande; for more details, contact the Milan Tourist Office (see page 123). A popular local festival is held along the *Darsena Ticinese* on the first Sunday in June (see page 91).

Giardini Pubblici

Just north of the city centre, the private gardens of the 18th-century aristocracy have been transformed into a delightful 17-hectare (42-acre) public park. Wide avenues of chestnut trees crisscross handsome landscaped gardens in the classical Italian style amidst rock banks and duck-populated ponds. For children, there is a host of pony-carts, a miniature train, and bumper cars.

Inside the park, the classical French-style **Villa Reale**, built in 1790 for the Belgioioso family, contains **The Modern Art Gallery**. You will find Italian futurists (the Italian movement that arose in 1909 and included Boccioni, Carrà, and Balla), sculpture by Marino Marini, and French 19th-century artists (among others Corot, Sisley, Manet, Cézanne, Gauguin, and Van Gogh).

The **Museo di Storia Naturale** (Natural History Museum), the largest in Italy, has a great collection of minerals, giant crystals, insects, fossils, and dinosaurs, as well as a library. Alternatively, you can always reach for the stars at the nearby **Planetarium**. On the far-west side of the park, in the Palazzo Dugnani, the **Cinema Museum** shows old cameras, projectors, and, best of all, films.

Stazione Centrale

Mussolini's promise to make the trains run on time found its architectural expression in Italy's largest railway station. *Stazione Centrale's* imposing mass and monstrous bombast is the perfect epitome of fascist design (1925–1931).

Compared with the aggressive façade, the interior is much more successful. It is built on a gigantic scale and designed to impress, but achieves its effects with panache, notably in the steel-and-glass vaulting over the platforms.

The man who inflated its Neo-Classical forms was Ulisse Stacchini. Fortunately, architects Giò di Ponti and Pierluigi Nervi were around in the 1950s to offset the damage with their sleekly elegant **Pirelli Building** (or *Grattacielo Pirelli*, the first skyscraper in Italy), which looks down on the station from across the Piazza Duca d'Aosta.

This 127-m- (416-ft-) high tower, 25 m (80 ft) wide, was erected to mark the site of Pirelli's first rubber factory and is now the seat of government for the whole region of

Lombardy. With its graceful sides tapering like a ship's bow, it was among the very first skyscrapers to abandon the standard, rectangular block design, using, instead, a revolutionary hexagonal structure.

Cimitero Monumentale

Not everyone thinks of a cemetery as a place to go sightseeing. This particular resting-place, however, is well worth the 15-minute taxi ride northwest of the Duomo for its amazing tributes in granite and marble to bourgeois Milanese pride and pathos.

When they say *monumentale*, they are not kidding. A Pharaonic pyramid, enormous Roman sarcophagus, lifesize crucifixion, and several other morbid but fascinating tributes vie for your attention. Nothing, it seems, is too good for the dearly departed Milanese. The centrerpiece is a gigantic Neo-Gothic temple sheltering the tomb of famous novelist Alessandro Manzoni, author of *I promessi sposi (The Betrothed),* along with busts of the revered Verdi—who wrote his *Requiem* in honor of Manzoni—and independence heroes Giuseppe Garibaldi and Camilo Cavour.

Soldiers are particularly well served, including a colonel sculpted with all his medals and a sergeant major being devoured by a Gorgon. Best of all is one Davide Campari who, before he died, commissioned a full size reproduction of Leonardo's *Last Supper* for his tomb. The guardians are usually pleased to show you where.

CITY EXCURSIONS

Although the towns of Pavia, Monza, and Bergamo can all be reached on easy day trips from Milan, they also make for good overnight trips. Bergamo, in particular, is a very pleasant stopover on the way to or from Lake Garda.

Certosa di Pavia

After the Milan Duomo itself, this great charterhouse, begun in the 15th century as a Visconti family mausoleum, is the most spectacular monument in the region. A 30-minute drive south of Milan, it can be visited independently of Pavia itself, which lies 7 km (4 miles) farther down the road.

Beyond the public entrance, the interior courtyard leading to the church has **wine cellars** and **food stores**, across from the Baroque **Palazzo Ducale**, which constitutes the prior's and ducal apartments.

For the monastery's church, Duke Gian Galeazzo Visconti used many of the masons and sculptors who were working on his cathedral in Milan (see page 17). The edifice marks a crucial point in the transition in styles from flamboyant Gothic to Renaissance. Even without the originally designed crowning gable, the sculpted marble **façade** has a dazzling impact. There are more than 70 statues of prophets, saints and apostles above the medallion reliefs of Roman emperors.

The Gothic interior, with its characteristic vaulting, is lightened-up with brightly colored pavements. Among the chapels, which were decorated in Baroque style in the late 16th century, notice in the north (left) aisle an exquisite Perugino altarpiece of *God the Father*. Right of the triumphant Baroque high altar are a finely carved 15th-century *lavabo* (ritual basin) and a delightful *Madonna and Child* by Bernardino Luini. In the south (right) transept is the **Visconti tomb**.

A door here leads to a small cloister of terracotta offering a good view of the church's galleried octagonal tower. The **Great Cloister** farther to the south boasts 122 arches, with similar terracotta decoration for the monks' 24 cells. In 1947, Cistercian monks took over from the Carthusians;

fortunately, they have continued the traditional manufacture of herbal liqueurs. Their **refectory** has glorious ceiling frescoes by Bergognone.

Pavia

The Lombards' first capital is now a sleepy, red-bricked university town (population 85,000), some 34 km (21 miles) south of Milan. Hurry through its modern suburbs to the attractive *centro storico*.

The Lombard kings established their court in Pavia in the sixth century (see page 13); French King Charlemagne was crowned Emperor here in 774, Frederick Barbarossa in 1155. Pavia was the birthplace (c.1005) of Lanfranc,

A fresco detail from the spectacular Certosa di Pavia, a 30-minute drive south of Milan.

first Archbishop of Canterbury under the Normans. The French have less happy memories of the city, since King François I was captured by Emperor Charles V in 1525 at the crucial battle of Pavia (in the northern outskirts at Mirabello) and imprisoned in Madrid.

The Spanish ramparts from the 17th century are visible along the northern edge of the city centre as you drive in from Milan. Start walking on the south side of town at the **Ponte Coperto** (Covered Bridge), which spans the Ticino river. The bridge has been reconstructed east of the medieval original, which was bombed in 1944. The Ticino descends from Switzerland via Lake Maggiore to join the Po southeast of Pavia.

From the picturesque riverside road, take the Via Diacono over to the **Church of San Michele**, the city's major Romanesque monument. Its octagonal dome was completed in 1155 for Emperor Frederick Barbarossa's crowning and the church was the site for all coronations thereafter. The simple sandstone façade is notable for its subtly sculpted friezes over the three recessed portals and an elegant band of 21 arches following the angle of the roof gable. The interior has superb rib vaulting over the nave and aisles and fine carving on the column capitals.

Head left on Corso Garibaldi and turn right along Strada Nuova, which traces the old Roman road's south–north axis from the Ponte Coperto. Behind the *Broletto* (town hall) is the late-15th-century **Duomo**, a Renaissance structure with details added by Bramante and Leonardo da Vinci. The dome dates from the 19th century but the façade was not completed until later, in 1933.

Back on Strada Nuova, cross the ancient Roman east–west axis (now Corso Mazzini and Corso Cavour), to pass the 18th-century buildings of the **University of Pavia**, on the right. The university was originally founded by the Lombards as the nation's foremost school of law, and was made a full university by the Visconti in 1361. Pavia's most celebrated teacher was Alessandro Volta (1745–1827), professor of physics and pioneer in electricity who gave his name to the unit of electric measurement. Napoleon bestowed on him the title of count.

A well conceived **museum** recounts the fascinating history of the university. On Piazza Leonardo da Vinci are three medieval **tower houses** of the Pavia nobility and beneath the square the 11th-century **crypt** of Sant' Eusebeio.

At the north end of Strada Nuova is the Visconti's formidable 14th-century fortress, **Castello Visconteo**. Its rear fourth side was lost in 1527, but there are two corner turrets remaining on the south side. Enter the fine terracotta arcaded courtyard for access to the **Museo Civico** (see page 65). Besides a small but interesting collection of Roman antiquities and Lombard sculpture, the **Pinacoteca** houses important works by Giovanni Bellini, Correggio, Boltraffio, Foppa, Tiepolo and the Netherlands painters Hugo Van der Goes and Lucas Van Leyden.

Over to the west (at the end of Via Griziotti), is the 12th-century church of **San Pietro in Ciel d'Oro**. It is revered as the last resting place of St. Augustine, whose relics are said to have been brought here from Carthage (near where he died in 430) and are now enshrined in the great Gothic, sculpted marble **Arca di Sant'Agostino** (1362). The Romanesque interior provides a simple setting for the grandiose monument. The *Ciel d'Oro* (golden ceiling) of the church's name refers to a now long-gone gilded vault. A verse from Dante's *Paradiso* is quoted on the façade in reference to the martyred Roman poet Boethius, who is buried in the crypt.

Monza

If you do not feel like driving through Milan's northeast industrial suburbs, it's an easy 30-minute bus ride from beside *Stazione Centrale* to this picturesque gingerbread town with a friendly population of 120,000. Monza, now the fabled home of Grand Prix motor racing (for ticketing details see page 89), was actually founded on hat and carpet manufacturing.

The track and grandstands take up some 15 percent of the lovely **Villa Reale park**, which covers 800 hectares (2,000 acres) in all. The land was confiscated from the aristocracy and handed over to the people in 1805 by Napoleon's stepson and viceroy in Italy, Eugène de Beauharnais. The English-style landscaped parkland is still dotted with patrician mansions and is home to the Austrian Archduke Ferdinand's Neo-Classical Villa Reale (1780), which stands among rose gardens and greenhouses.

This is great picnic country and caters to all forms of sport: tennis, golf (Milan Golf Club has 18- and 9-hole courses), polo, field hockey, swimming, skating, hiking, and jogging. Bicycles can also be rented in the park. Wild stag, hare, and pheasant roam freely, some all the way onto the woodlands in the middle of the racetrack. Horse races were held at the Mirabello hippodrome until it fell under disrepair.

Historically, Monza was an important city of the Lombard kings. The Gothic **cathedral** is older than Milan's, and is notable for its 13th-century white-and-green marble façade and Pellegrino Tibaldi's brick campanile (1605). The church was founded in A.D. 595 by the Lombard Queen Theodelinda, whose tomb is in the **Capella Zavattari** to the left of the high altar. Inside the church's **Museo Serpero** downstairs is the Lombards' **Iron Crown**, used in the coronation both of Holy Roman Emperors and Napoleon himself (as king of Italy; see page 20). It is so called because it is said to contain a piece of iron from one of the nails used to hammer Jesus to the cross. Theodelinda's treasure also includes ancient silver, ivory, embroidery, silk, and other religious relics.

Bergamo

Rising out of the plain of the Po valley around its own steep little hill, roughly 47 km (30 miles) northeast of Milan, the delightful town of Bergamo makes a welcome break in the monotony of the *autostrada*. Divided into lower and upper cities (*Città Bassa* and *Alta* respectively), the population of 122,000 earns a living from fabric manufacturing and the metal industry. It has a proud soldiering history, having given the Venetian Republic a famous *condottiere,* Bartolomeo Colleoni, and the largest contingent in Garibaldi's 1,000 Red Shirts for the *Risorgimento*. A funicular links the two parts of the city along with a winding road, but it is advisable to go without a car as traffic is limited.

Città Bassa

The Lower City is the modern town of shops, hotels, and restaurants serving local specialties such as *polenta e osei*, creamy corn porridge, and roasted local birds. Marcello Piacentini creatively laid out the area with style and panache in the early 20th century along airy, broad boulevards and squares, before he succumbed to the demands of Mussolini as official architect of the Fascist State.

The main street, Viale Giovanni XXIII, leads to Piazza Matteotti and the hub of the town's lively café scene along the tree-lined **Sentierone** arcades. Opposite is the 18th-century **Teatro Donizetti** and a monument showing the Bergamo-born opera composer accompanied by the naked lady he is always said to have needed for inspiration.

At the eastern end of the piazza, step inside the church of **San Bartolomeo** to look at Lorenzo Lotto's fine altar painting (1516). Climbing to the Upper City, farther east, **Via Pignolo** is most notable for its elegant 16th- to 18th-century palazzi and the church of **Santo Spirito**, with a fine polyptych by Bergognone.

Città Alta is home to some of Bergamos's most distinguished buildings.

Città Alta

The recently restructured Venetian walls, which can be toured from above or within a series of secret passageways, still protect the historic Upper City on the 366-m- (1,200-ft-) tall hill. "Alta," meaning "high," refers to the city's altitude, 400 m (1,300 ft) above sea level. The gracious **Piazza Vecchia** is surrounded by a vast number of Renaissance public edifices —notably the **Palazzo della Ragione** with a medieval tower, Torre del Comune. Take the lift to enjoy the rooftop view over the Po valley to the Alps.

The town's most venerable edifice, on Piazza del Duomo, is the 12th-century Romanesque church of **Santa Maria Maggiore**. Notice the finely carved, monumental porch and slender campanile. The Baroque interior has impressive 16th-century **tapestries** and Donizetti's tomb on the west wall. The inlaid **choir stalls** and intarsia on the altar rail include designs by Lorenzo Lotto. Also note the beautiful wooden confessional by Andrea Fantoni.

Adjacent to the church is the Renaissance **Colleoni Chapel**, the *condottiere*'s extravagant mausoleum in red, white, and green marble. The lavish façade illustrating classical and Biblical allegory is no masterpiece, but it gives wonderful expression to the old soldier's legendary braggadocio. Some of the windows' pillars reproduce the shape

The beautiful Borromeo Islands, as viewed from the scenic heights of nearby Stresa.

of cannon barrels that Colleoni pioneered on the battlefield. Inside is his tomb, a gilded wooden equestrian statue, and ceiling frescoes by Tiepolo.

A short walk from the Città Alta's Porta Sant'Agostino, the recently restructured **Galleria dell'Accademia Carrara** stands on the northeast side of the Lower City. It includes a *Madonna and Child* by Mantegna, and paintings by Bellini, Lotto, Raphael, Titian, Botticelli, and Carpaccio. Among the foreign artists represented are Holbein, Rubens, Velázquez, Rembrandt, and El Greco. In front of the Galleria, is a **Modern Art Museum** – the former was restored and the latter created for the Jubilee 2000.

THE LAKES

Italy's most famous lakes—Maggiore, Como, and Garda—are within easy reach of Milan. A popular destination with the Italians themselves, they are at their best, and busiest, in spring, when the luxuriant vegetation is in full bloom.

Lake Maggiore

Blessed with a temperate, mild climate and luxuriant vegetation, Lake Maggiore is a watery arm curving along the foot of the Alps, 64 km (40 miles) long and nearly 5 km (3 miles) at its widest point, with the "elbow" at Baveno. With the Ticino river as its main affluent, it covers 212 sq km (82 square miles), one fifth of it being at the Locarno (northern) end, in Switzerland.

Since 1748, the west shore has been part of the Piedmont region, but it has never lost its identity as part of Lombardy since the domination of the Visconti in the Middle Ages and the presence of the Borromeo family from the 15th century.

The family dynasty, which gave Milan its greatest cardinals, also gave its name to the lake's romantic islands—the

A palazzo on Isola Bella, an island named after Isabella, wife of Count Carlo Borromeo.

Borromean Islands. These are still owned by the family, as are the lake's fishing rights.

Trains from Milan's *Stazione Nord* take one hour to Arona at the lake's southern end or 90 minutes to Laveno on the eastern shore.

Varese

With its own little lake, *Lago di Varese*, nearby this pleasant town was founded on the shoe-manufacturing industry (which sadly did not survive to see the 21st century). It is located 56 km (35 miles) northwest of Milan and makes a convenient stop for drivers heading for the Laveno car ferry at Lake Maggiore. Pick up some typical Varese snacks for the ride at the locally famous Panifico Trainini (Via Sacco, 12).

The handsome public gardens (**Giardini Pubblici**) offer a great view north to the nearby Alps, beyond the fine Baroque **Palazzo Estense** that serves as the town hall. Laid out in classically Italian style, the beautiful gardens harbor the 18th-century Villa Mirabello, home to the **Museo Civico** (municipal museum), which is a small museum devoted to local affairs. The museum's collection includes various antiquities unearthed from thoughout the surrounding area and a selection of paintings by historic artists from Varese.

☛ *Borromean Islands*

Close to the western shore of Lake Maggiore, the *Isole Borromee* are celebrated for their Baroque palazzi and magnificent gardens. All are within easy reach by boat from Stresa, Baveno or Pallanza.

A statue reposes in a palazzo garden on Isola Bella.

Isola Bella is named after Isabella, wife of Count Carlo Borromeo, who planned the island haven for her. The soil in its ten tiers of terraced gardens had to be brought by barge from the mainland.

In addition to admirable works by Annibale Carracci, Tiepolo, Zuccarelli, and Giordano, the 17th-century **palazzo** is decorated with landscape paintings by Antonio Tempesta, who used the island as a refuge after being accused of murdering his wife.

There is a wonderful collection of 18th-century puppets in the basement. The terraced gardens constitute one of the finest examples of the Italian formal style. View the lake from the uppermost terrace, by the unicorn statue that is the Borromeo family emblem.

Isola dei Pescatori (Fishermen's Island) is, indeed, simply a peaceful fishing village with tiny, narrow streets and a pleasant little restaurant that makes this a particularly pleasant outing.

Isola Madre, farther out in the lake, is the largest of the islands. The **botanical gardens** set around the 16th-century palazzo here are renowned for their rhododendrons, camellias (April) and azaleas (May), as well as resident pheasants and raucous white peacocks all year round.

☛ *Stresa*

Since the 19th century, and particularly since the construction of Napoleon's Simplon Road through the Alps, Stresa has been the lake's principal resort, boasting the most luxurious hotels. The lakeside **Lungolago promenade** is famous for its flowers and bewitching views of the islands. On the southern outskirts, in the **Villa Pallavicino** (1850), visit the beautiful, hillside botanical gardens which occupy sprawling parkland laid out in English, French and Italian style.

You can also take the cable car up to the peak of the **Mottarone** (at a vertiginously high 1,491 m/4,892 ft), from where there are exhilarating views of the Lombardy lakes, the Alps, and Po valley. Alternatively, a free piece of the toll road will get you there via the **Giardino Alpinia** (Alpine Gardens), displaying an impressive 2,000 varieties of mountain plants.

Verbania

Just around the "elbow" of Lake Maggiore from Stresa, this handsome resort shares, along with neighbouring **Pallanza** and **Intra**, a microclimate of hot summers and gloriously mild winters that support a carefully nurtured, semi-tropical vegetation. The town takes its name from the vervain tea herb that grows rampant here (as do fragrant magnolias).

Just north of Verbania with a direct service by boat, **Villa Taranto** offers the lake's most spectacular **botanical gardens** (open from April to October). The 16 hectares (40 acres) of parkland were bequeathed to Italy in 1931 by Scottish soldier Captain Neil McEacharn. Among the fountains, waterfalls, basins and lily ponds, you will find several thousand varieties of plants. They have been brought to these gardens from all over the world and gradually acclimatized here over the years. This is the only place apart from the Nile valley where some Egyptian plants will grow.

Baveno

North of Stresa, this quieter little resort was visited by Queen Victoria, who promenaded here when staying at the nearby Castello Bianco. Baveno is famous for its local red-and-white granite used in the construction of St. Peter's basilica in Rome. The octagonal, Renaissance **baptistery** on the main square and the 12th-century **parish church** are both worth a look.

Locarno and Ascona (Switzerland)

Don't forget your passport if you intend on crossing the border into the Swiss part of the lake. (The last town on the Italian side, Cannobio, is famous for its anti-smuggling flotilla of *torpediere* boats.) Locarno is one of the very few places in the Alpine country where you can see unlikely subtropical foliage such as banana plants, date palms, and orange trees.

Milan's lords once vacationed on these very shores, as is testified by the handsome remains of the **Castello Visconti**. Its 15th-century courtyard, surrounded by graceful arcades, leads to the **Museo Civico**, which harbors a rich archaeological collection that includes many notable Roman relics.

A few streets away is the airy, curving **Piazza Grande**, the city's main square. Its arcades offset Locarno's annual International Film Festival, during which films are shown on an outdoor screen.

Uphill from the Piazza is the **Città Vecchia**, the old town of stately villas, timeworn apartment buildings, hidden gardens, and venerable churches. Among the turreted mansions, look out for **Casa Rusca** in Piazza Sant'Antonio, containing the art collection donated by French-born sculptor Jean Arp, a founder of the Dada Movement and leading Surrealist. He died here in 1966.

A five-minute funicular ride from the center of town leads to the sanctuary of **Madonna del Sasso**, perched on its steep rock. For centuries, pilgrims have traveled on foot to pray at the site of a miraculous vision in the church. From the church, you can take a cable car and then a chair lift to the **Cimetta** belvedere, giving a superb panorama of both town and lake.

Ascona is separated from Locarno by the Maggia river flowing into the lake. Once a simple fishing village, it has become popular with artists and writers. Favoured in the past by dancer Isadora Duncan, painter Paul Klee, and the exiled Lenin, it now hosts frequent art exhibitions and an annual festival of classical music. The **lake promenade** has lively outdoor cafés and restaurants, and Swiss jewellery shops and Italian fashion boutiques occupy the side streets.

Lake Como

Embraced by green wooded escarpments, the lake frequented by some of England's most romantic 19th-century poets, including Wordsworth, Shelley, and Byron, retains a certain wistful atmosphere for the leisure hours of the Milanese and lake-lovers from beyond the Alps.

Its three elongated arms meet at the promontory of its principal resort, Bellagio. The main river feeding the lake is the Adda, flowing in from the north and through the south-east arm at Lecco, the last stronghold of Como's old-fashioned *lucie* fishing boats. Trains from Milan to the town of Como take about an hour, making this a possible day trip.

Como

For centuries known as a silk-manufacturing centre, Como (population 50,000) lies 49 km (30 miles) up the A9 *autostrada* from Milan. The *centro storico* retains the checkerboard plan of the ancient Roman town of Comum. Also famous for its library and schools, Como was the home of classical writers Pliny the Elder (who died while observing the volcanic eruption of Mt. Vesuvius that engulfed Pompeii on 24 August A.D. 79) and his nephew and adopted son, Pliny the Younger (A.D. 62–120).

Como's other famous son, 18th-century electricity pioneer Alessandro Volta, is honored with a monument which stands appropriately in *Piazza Volta*. The Neo-Classical **Tempio Volta** in the lakefront **Giardini Pubblici** (Public Gardens) displays the scientific instruments, namely the battery, with which he developed the "volt" as a unit of electrical measurement.

Sailboats moored on Lake Como suggest the potential for adventure —for those who can afford it.

The **Lungo Lario** lakefront promenade is the natural setting for the town's *passeggiata* in the late afternoon, past the cruise-boats' landing stage, and the hotels, cafés and restaurants on the **Piazza Cavour**, popular meeting place in the evenings. It is also the backdrop for the first Italian produced soap opera *Vivere.*

A distinctive cupola crowns the Gothic-Renaissance cathedral in Como.

The town's handsome, Gothic-Renaissance **cathedral** (15th century) is crowned by a superb Baroque dome added in 1744 by Turin's great architect, Filippo Juvarra. On the façade, both Elder and Younger Pliny are portrayed in seated sculptures on either side of the central doorway. In the lofty Gothic interior, notice the nine 16th-century **tapestries** in the nave, in the south (right) aisle chapels, altar paintings by Bernardino Luini, in particular *The Holy Conversation.* Next to the cathedral is the arcaded 13th-century **Broletto** (town hall) in white, grey and pink marble.

Most of the shops in town offer fashions for both men and women, as well as accessories from the area's celebrated silk mills, still supplying everyone from Valentino's haute couture line to the Vatican with some of the world's finest silk products.

☛ *Bellagio*

This tranquil resort juts out into the lake on a hilly promontory. Up on the heights above the town, the elegant 18th-century **Villa Serbelloni** (not to be confused with the Villa Serbelloni luxury hotel down near the lakefront) stands in the middle of a beautiful park of rose trees, camellias, magnolias and pomegranates open to the public. At the southern end of town, the **lido** offers a bracing swim.

Lake cruises and the car ferry leave from the Lungolago Marconi. When looking for gifts, remember that Bellagio craftsmen are also renowned for their silk weaving as well as olive-wood carving.

The Hotel Villa Serbelloni looks onto Lake Como.

Excursions around Lake Como

Lake Como's most attractive stretch of water is its southwest arm. If you're based at Bellagio, the only way to see the colorful grottoes and misty waterfall at **Nesso** is by taking a boat cruise south from Lezzeno. The western shore of the lake is lined with villas that are nestled in fragrant gardens.

At **Cernobbio**, just north of Como, the 16th-century Villa d'Este is now one of the world's most fabled hotels (see page 131) where you can "take tea" and stroll among its manicured grounds spotted with cypresses and magnolias.

The lake's temperate climate encourages the hotel's lush gardens.

Between the genteel resort towns of **Tremezzo** and **Cadenabbia**, you'll find one of the lake's most beautiful residences (open to the public), the 18th-century **Villa Carlotta**. There's a marvelous view of the lake from its lovely terraced gardens, which are famous for their display of camellias, azaleas and rhododendrons in late April and May.

Lake Garda

Surrounded by rolling green hills, Lake Garda is graced with vineyards (notably those of Bardolino), lemon trees, olive groves and noble cedars. People seeking a restful holiday enjoy its mild winters and mellow summers, and Garda has long been popular with visitors from Austria, Switzerland, and Germany.

On the west shore, the people of Salò, where Gasparo Bertolotti is said to have designed the violin, suggest his inspiration came from the contours of the lake. Italy's largest lake is shaped less like a violin than a banjo, however, measuring 52 km (32 miles) from the cliffs at the tip of its neck down to the base of the broad "sound box". At its widest, it stetches 18 km (11 miles); its surface is 370 square km (143 square miles).

A view over the fishing village/spa town of Sirmione from the amazing Rocca Scaligera

The town of Brescia is the most convenient of the large towns on the way to Garda, just under a half an hour, with rail and *autostrada* links to the resort town of Desenzano del Garda, some 118 km (73 miles) from Milan.

Brescia

Made famous for weapons manufacturing (notably the world famous Biretta guns), Brescia suffered as an obvious target in World War II, but has rebounded as an ebullient modern city (population 200,000) with a well-preserved and restored *centro storico* based around the **Piazza del Duomo**. Since 1927 the piazza has been the site for the starting and finishing point of one of Europe's most exciting vintage car rallies, the *1000 Miglia* held each May.

The most interesting of the piazza's two churches is not the present cathedral—a rather ponderous, 17th-century affair—but its Romanesque predecessor, the large, brick Duomo Vecchio, usually known as the **Rotonda**. Inside this round, 11th-century building are a series of notable paintings by Moretto da Brescia, including *The Assumption* over the high altar and, in the choir, *St Luke, St Mark, Elijah Asleep,* and the *Sacrifice of Isaac*.

The delightful **Piazza della Loggia** is valiantly resisting the brutal, modern office blocks that tower above the neighboring Piazza della Vittoria, the latter being severe examples of Piacentini's architecture after he was employed by Mussolini.

At the western end of the square is the handsome 16th-century **town hall** *(Loggia)*, graced with an early Renaissance pawnshop, **Monte di Pietà**, now a commercial space, on the south side.

The art collection of the **Pinacoteca Tosio-Martinengo** (Via Martinengo da Barco) is devoted principally to

Brescia's own resident Renaissance masters—Moretto, Foppa, Romanino, and Savoldo—but the museum also has fine works by such undisputed Renaissance masters as Raphael, Lotto and Tintoretto.

Desenzano del Garda

This lively resort is the gateway to Lake Garda. Plan your itinerary at a café in the attractive, arcaded **Piazza Capelletti** on the lakefront, or simply watch the world go by.

The nearby parish church of **Santa Maria Maddelena** has a *Last Supper* by Tiepolo in its Chapel of the Sacrament, while in the Via degli Scavi are the ruins of a **Roman villa**.

Sirmione

Perched on a narrow promontory, the fishing village and renowned spa and resort of Sirmione offers a unique view of the lake. At the tip of the promontory in a romantic setting of olive trees are the **Grotte di Catullo**, the vaulted ruins of a Roman villa. They are often attributed to the ancient poet Catullus, who had his summer residence at Sirmione in the first century B.C. Fresco fragments from the same period can be seen in the site's remarkable **Antiquarium**.

One of the best vantage points in town is the tower of the 13th-century castle, **Rocca Scaligera**, built out onto the water beside the town gate by the Scaligeri lords of nearby Verona.

Sirmione's *Stazione Termale* (spa) on the northern edge of town is here to help restore tired bones and muscles, skin problems, and breathing, from March to November.

The Boiola sulphur springs, famous since ancient Roman times, rise from the lake bed just north of the peninsula at a temperature of 69°C (156°F).

Gardesana Occidentale (West Shore)

The well-known drive along the winding road cut through the cliffs of the lake's west shore is one of the most spectacular in Italy.

The eye-pleasing resort town of **Salò** is set in a narrow bay. With its historical museum contained within the 16th-century Palazzo della Magnifica Patria, it attempts to live down its regrettable moment as the capital of Mussolini's puppet republic, which was installed here by the Germans in September 1943.

The Rocca Scaligera was built right out onto the water.

☛ **Gardone Riviera** is a fashionable resort much appreciated for its parks and botanical gardens, and as base for hikes up and around **Monte Lavino**.

Above the town, in Gardone di Sopra, is a 20th-century "folly", **Il Vittoriale**, the bizarre and disturbing residence of Gabriele d'Annunzio, poet, adventurer, and Fascist. Melancholy gardens of dense shrubbery, dark laurel and parades of cypresses lead past a Greek theatre to a mausoleum with the writer's green marble sarcophagus flanked by those of his disciples. It overlooks the prow of a World War I warship, the *Puglia*, which was hauled up the hillside as the *pièce de résistance* of this macabre villa-museum. The villa houses two cars in which d'Annunzio drove himself to the World War I battlefront and the aircraft from which he dropped his propaganda leaflets over Vienna. His library includes a collection of precious 16th-century books, rare manuscripts and also an Austrian machine gun.

Il Vittoriale, the strange villa-museum devoted to writer Gabriele d'Annunzio.

Gardesana Orientale (East Shore)

The southeastern corner of Lake Garda, which belongs to the province of Verona in the Veneto region, can be visited on a boat trip. First port of call from Sirmione is the historic resort town of **Peschiera**, which has retained old ramparts from its late days as a stronghold of the Venetian empire. **Bardolino**, which is world-famous for its lusty red wines, boasts the remains of a Scaligeri castle and also two picturesque medieval churches, the ninth-century San Zeno and 12th-century San Severo.

The town of **Garda** has a lovely promenade, while 3 km (2 miles) further west is the cypress-lined headland of **Punta San Vigilio**. From here, in the Villa Guarnienti's Italian-style gardens, you can enjoy one of the lake's loveliest views.

WHAT TO DO

There are plenty of things to do other than sightseeing in and around Milan and the lakes. We offer some suggestions here for shopping, entertainment, sports and what to do with the kids.

SHOPPING

Milan and the lake resorts are full of great buys, but don't expect to find too many bargains. The Milanese know the value of their design sense and put an appropriate price on it. One intriguing comeback due to the economic crisis of the 1990s is the ancient art of bargaining — although it's much subtler nowadays. Make a discreet inquiry about a possible *sconto* (discount), and you may get a pleasant surprise.

Markets

There are 10 or 12 common street markets in Milan set up from 8:30am to 1pm each day in different neighbourhoods. Here you can buy anthing from fruits and vegetables to fashion footwear knock-offs to second hand clothing to kitchen gadgets. Ask the Tourist information office (see page 123) for a full list of addresses. Every Saturday from 8:30am to 5pm you will find one of the largest, the *Fiera di Senigallia,* on Viale G. D'Annunzio, along the **Darsena basin** with a wide assortment of wares.

The most popular antiques market takes place on the nearby Via Ripa Porta Ticinese along the **Naviglio Grande** on the last Sunday of each month (except for July). Venders begin to set up at dawn – the best time for anyone looking for a good deal to get there – and tend to close after lunch hour. More chic (and expensive) is the **Brera** neighborhood antique market on the third Saturday of each month at Via

Fiori Chiari, Via Madonnina, and Piazza Formentini. It starts a little later (10am), but some vendors stay well past dusk. Outside Milan, **Bergamo** (see page 60) holds a mixed flea market in the Upper City's Piazza Vecchia on the third Sunday of the month. **Pavia** (see page 56) has an antiques market every first Sunday except January and August.

What to Buy

Antiques: The Via Montenapoleone and Brera districts (see page 45) are the heart of the antiques-dealers' territory. Of the many interesting and respectable choices, try: L'Oro dei Farlocchi at 5 Via Madonnina for Italian **Medieval and Baroque furniture**; on 22 Via Spiga, visit Subert for **scientific instruments**; and, at 46 Via Spiga, Brucoli offers a selection of beautiful antique **jewellery**.

Clothes: Milan is Italy's undisputed fashion capital and the centuries-old Italian sense of style and colour quite often is the source of inspiration for designs seen in Paris, New York, and Tokyo. Some designer clothes may be cheaper back home, but you will find a much greater selection here and the latest styles are aften

Peruse the best boutiques on Via Montenapoleone.

shown in Milanese stores first. For both women's and men's clothes, the master couturiers Versace, Prada, Armani, Moschino, Missoni, Fendi, Gucci, Ermenegildo Zegna and Gianfranco Ferré all have their boutiques on and around the celebrated "Montenapo", principally along Via Montenapoleone itself and its off-shoots such as Via della Spiga and Via Sant'Andrea.

For the best in Italian **shoes,** try Cesare Paciotti, Ferragamo, Bruno Magli and Fratelli Rossetti; for **lingerie**, Pratesi or La Perla; for exclusive **beachwear**, Cavallini; for the softest, most exquisite **leather**, Gucci, Bottega Veneto and Nazareno Gabrielli. **Children's fashion** can be found around the city at Prenatal. **Fiorucci** in the Gallery Passarella at San Babila is a Milanese icon with the latest high fashion casual wear, household gadgets and other fun accessories for the young customer. There is also the possibility to buy **second hand** high fashion from Mercatino Michela, with five locations (Tel. 02/799748 for addresses) in the form of "sample sales". Die-hard bargain shoppers should take time to seek out

A colourful market reflects Milan's bounty of fine food.

You might be surprised at the abundance of local goods, in addition to souvenirs, you can find at open markets.

special **outlets** in Milan and its suburbs. Ask the Tourist Information office for a full listing.

Cosmetics: You can find **handmade cosmetics**, soaps and fragrances at Lusc at 6 Via Fiori Chiari in Brera. Another source of natural and creative **hair- and bodycare products,** is an erborista, such as the *Centro Erboristico Milanese* at 3 Via Melzo.

Craftwork: The quality of traditional craftsmanship outside Milan can still be admired in the ornaments and utensils of wrought iron, turned wood, and embossed copper at the pretty city of Bergamo. Lake Maggiore resorts are especially known for Arona ceramics, Como and Bellagio for silk and carved olive wood, and Brescia for hunting rifles.

Gourmet Foods: In Milan, the great gift specialty is the gargantuan *panettone* — a sweet, egg-based holiday loaf with raisins (see page 97). You will find them most commonly before and during the Christmas season displayed in any fine *pasticceria*. There are many small speciality food shops all over the city and the resort areas carrying local specialities. You will find the largest selection of producers for regional products sold in their native area; for example if you plan to visit Lake Garda, wait to make your olive oil purchase there. For a full array of other Lombardy specialities

While known primarily as a fashion centre, Milan is also known for its antiques, including exquisite jewellery.

visit the famous **Peck**, Via Speronari 3 (Metro: Duomo), which has just combined all of their little shops into one large, two-storied centre. Go upstairs and grab a table to sit and enjoy the delicacies that have caught your eye.

Household Accessories: Milan has an unrivalled range of innovative styles in everything from fountain pens and lamps to kitchenware, espresso machines and other household gadgets. The best known household gadget designer is **Alessi** with its own store at 9 Corso Matteotti. More serious Italian kitchenware afficionados should visit the **Medagliani** warehouse store in the small mall at Via San Gregorio 43. **G. Lorenzi** in Via Montenapoleone 9 carries a fine selection of knives and other tableware.

Jewellery: The country's top jewellers share the "Montenapo" district with the fashion designers. The leading shops are: Bulgari, Buccellati, Calderoni, Jacente and Dal Vecchio (for antique jewels).

Lake Garda's goldsmiths are highly respected, with boutiques at all the major resorts, and Brescia is known for its fine silverware. For upmarket designer watches, many take the cruise on Lake Maggiore across the Swiss frontier to Locarno, where you'll find the greatest selection. Otherwise, try **Centro P. R. Lorenz** at 12 Via Montenapoleone in central Milan.

Modern Furniture: Even if you're not contemplating carrying an armchair home, it can be interesting to do some astute window shopping in Milan to help place early orders with distributors back where you live. The major stores of international fame are conveniently grouped along Via Manzoni. For the hottest new kitchens the Boffi showroom is on the nearby Via Solferino 11. Otherwise on your way up to Como, stop in the B&B Italia showroom; Strada Provinciale 32, Novedrate (Co); Tel 031/795111.

Textiles: Como and its environs have been renowned as a silk-producing hub for centuries. For generations its looms have produced the highest-quality silks, used for fashion, accessories and home furnishings for top-drawer clients as diverse as designer fashion house Prada and the Pope. In Como, the retail outlet of the world-famous Ratti factory, based at Via Cernobbi 17, on the road to the Villa d'Este Hotel, offers a wide selection of silks.

Toys: Long before Geppetto made Pinocchio, Italian toys, especially puppets, had their own magic. For the delight of children, try a few of the best Milan shops, namely: Cagnoni, Corso Vercelli 38 (Metro: Conciliazione); Giocattoli e Giochi, Città del Sole, Via Orefici 5 (Metro: Cairoli); and Toys Center, Via Mauro Macchi 29 (near Stazione Centrale).

ENTERTAINMENT

During the extensive renovation of La Scala (see page 34), **opera** is being performed at the newly built **Teatro degli Arcimboldi**, in zona Bicocca northwest of the station. Information on the current season and tickets is available on the La Scala website <www.teatroallascala.org>. Traditionally, Milan's opera season opens with a gala première on St Ambrose's feast day, on December 7 – if you are offered a ticket for this occasion, jump at the chance. Ballet is also performed at the Teatro degli Arcimboldi throughout the season.

Classical music concerts are much in demand in cultural Milan, most notably at the Teatro Filodrammatici, e-mail <filodrammatici@tiscilinet.it> , located near La Scala, on Via Filodrammatici; and at the Auditorium di Milano Orchestra Sinfonica G. Verdi, <www.orchestrasinfonica.milano.it>, on Via Torricelli.

Ballet is also staged at the Teatro Nazionale, <www.teatronazionale.com>, Piazza Piemonte 12.

Open-air concerts are regularly held in summer in Milan – at the Castello Sforzesco's Piazza d'Armi – as well as in the various lake resorts. Bergamo's delightful Teatro Donizetti makes an attractive venue for fine opera, ballet and classical music performances.

Even if your Italian is not up to scratch, for **theatre** it may still be worth your while attending one of the lively productions presented at the world-renowned Piccolo Teatro–Teatro Grassi; <www.piccoloteatro.org>; Via Rovello 2, created by the great Giorgio Strehler. The troupe's communicative style should transcend any language problems.

On the west side of town, the Palalido and Palazzetto dello Sport present large-scale **jazz** and **rock music** concerts. Palatrussardi, on Via S. Elia, also stages a variety of major musical events.

You can enjoy music in a more intimate setting, over a drink, at the bars in the Navigli (canal) quarters, to the southwest of the city.

La Scala, closed for restoration until late 2004.

This area really comes into its own at night, when the multitude of bars and restaurants alongside Milan's network of canals offer extensive drinking and dining options. Or, do as the Milanese do and take a civilised evening promenade along here.

The Tunnel on Via Sammartini 30 behind Stazione Centrale has live music on the weekends with a D.J. afterwards. If you are looking for a pub type atmosphere (Italian style) try Bar Magenta at the corner of Corso Magenta and Via Carducci (Metro: Cadorna), which boasts an abundant spread during the aperitif hour and sandwiches and snacks throughout the night.

A boat ride on beautiful Lake Maggiore makes a wonderful afternoon outing for the entire family.

Stop off at Caffe' della Pusterla on Via de Amicis 24 where the bartender will entertain you while preparing a cocktail then head off to one of Milan's many **clubs** such as Hollywood or Shocking, both near Stazione Garibaldi.

SPORTS

As in all Italian cities, soccer is king, but there are plenty of other sporting activities offered as well. For more detailed information about access to Milan's sporting facilities, contact Milanosport, Piazza Diaz 1A; Tel. 02/801466, fax 02/801460. Ask for a copy of their guide for a full listing of all available facilities.

Many of the resort hotels at the lakes have their own tennis courts and swimming pools. Inquire upon booking.

Tennis and Golf: The most easily accessible tennis courts (covered and open, hard and clay) from the city center are those at the Lido di Milano, Piazzale Lotto 15 (Metro Lotto); Tel. 02/39266100. Golf Club Milano's 9- and 18-hole courses are located in Monza's Villa Reale Park, entrance at Porta San Giorgio; Tel. 039/303081. Check first with the Milan tourist information office about temporary club membership. (The Monza park also has tennis courts and facilities for swimming, field hockey, and polo.)

Baseball and Basketball: Appropriate to its name, the Centro Sportivo Kennedy, Via Olivieri 15 Tel. 02/47996783, has a very respectable baseball diamond, while the Lido di Milano boasts a good basketball court.

Swimming and Watersports: The Lido di Milano also has a heated indoor pool (as well as a **gymnasium** for a preswimming workout). A little further out at the Parco Forlanini on the east side of town, the Saini sports center, Via Corelli 136, has the above plus an open-air pool.

Swimming in the lakes can be a very bracing affair, but the major resorts do offer amenities for **water-skiing, wind-surfing**, and **sailing**. For details of **fishing** in the lakes, enquire at local tourist information offices.

Spectator Sports: There can be few more exciting sporting spectacles in Europe than a **football** (soccer) match out at the Meazza Stadium (San Siro), Via Piccolomini 5. The city's two teams, AC Milan and Inter, are among the strongest in the world. All their games involve high drama but when the two teams play against each other, all eyes are on the field.

There is also **horse-racing** to watch at the San Siro race course, while **ice-hockey** matches take place at the Palazzo del Ghiaccio, Via Piranesi 14 (Stazione Porta Vittoria).

Motor rallies are held during the summer months around Bergamo, Brescia and Como. The region's biggest sporting event remains the **Grand Prix** Formula 1 motor race at Monza in September (see page 59).

MILAN WITH CHILDREN

The secret to keeping children amused in Milan is to make the most of the city's sights, even if they're not geared specifically towards kids. At the **Duomo,** for instance, a visit to the cathedral roof is always a great success. Also popular are Leonardo da Vinci's inventions at the **Science Museum** (see page 43). Taking to the water is usually a successful ploy: in Milan itself there are **canal cruises** on the Navigli, although more interesting are countless boat trips up and down the shores of the Lombard lakes. Youngsters may also enjoy the sports museum located at the stadium at San Siro; (Tel. 02/4042432).

Parks: Milan has two very large parks in close proximity to the city centre. Behind the Castello Sforzesco. **Parco**

Sempione (Metro: Lanza) provides lots of space for the kids to run around and let off steam. Besides its tropical fish, the **aquarium** (Via Gadio 2) has a wonderful collection of creepy, crawly reptiles. In August, the park hosts a summer festival, *Vacanze a Milano* (Vacation in Milan), offering free theatre and musical shows, dancing and open-air restaurants.

In the **Giardini Pubblici** (Metro: Palestro), you will find duck ponds, pony-rides, bumper cars and a miniature train. There is also a **Planetarium** here and dinosaurs in the **Natural History Museum**.

Puppets: Not far from the Science Museum is the Teatro delle Marionette, a delightful, privately run puppet theatre at Via Olivetani 3B; Tel. 02/4694440 (Metro: Conciliazione). When visiting the Borromean Islands on Lake Maggiore (see page 63), visit the 18th-century puppets in the palazzo on Isola Bella. And you can always head for Milan's toyshops (see page 85).

Special Events: Every Saturday morning **stamp** and **coin collectors** gather to exchange treasures on the Piazza degli Affari by the *Borso* (Stock Exchange, Metro: Cordusio). You will find bargain buys within pocket-money range. A **plant, flower and small animal** market is held on Sunday morning in front of the Palazzo Reale, from March to June and from September to December.

In the spring, kids may want to take their dads to the **Monza Motorcycle Grand Prix**. Call the Monza Autodromo; Tel. 039/2482212 or visit <www.monzanet.it> for more information, including dates and times.

For a sampling of other annual festive occasions, see the Calendar of Events on the opposite page; exact dates and other details are available from Tourist Information (see page 123).

Calendar of Events

Details of trade and fashion shows held at Milan's sprawling Fair Grounds (Metro: Amendola Fiera) are available from Ente Fiera Milano, Largo Domodossola 1, 20145 Milano; Tel. 02/49977908; fax 02/ 48193029; <www.fieramilano.com>.

January: Milan. 6 January, *Corteo dei Rei* Magi (Twelfth Night) procession between Sant'Ambrogio and Sant'Eustorgio.

February: Sei Giorni di Ciclismo (Six Days of Cycling) at forum di Assago; Tel. 02/488571; <www.filaforum.it>.

February/March: All cities. Carnival. Street parade, parties.

March: Milan. Via Crema; also Piacenza. 13 March *Tredesin de Marz* Flower festival marking the day children get their winter hair cut. Antique Book Exhibition International Trade Fair.

April: Bruzzano. *Palio della Suca,* small horse race in traditional Renaissance costumes.

May: Legnano. Last Sunday. Medieval-costumed battle and pageant commemorating the 1176 Lombard victory (see page 14). Brescia: *1000 Miglia* vintage car rally.

May-June: Bergamo and Brescia. International piano festival.

June: Milan. Navigli canal district festival; Comacina. Fireworks over Lake Como for midsummer Island Feast of *San Giovanni.*

July: Besana Brianza. First Sunday. *Festa di S. Camillo* celebrated at a Visconti villa with music and fireworks in the evening.

August: Milan. Vacanze a *Milano festival in Parco Sempione;* Gardone. Sailing regatta on Lake Garda.

August-September: Stresa. *Settimane Musicale,* music festival in churches and on Isola Bella.

September: Monza. Grand Prix Formula I motor racing; Como. *Autunno Musicale* international music festival (until November); Pavia. *Mostro Autunno* Pavese, gastronomic festival

October: Milan. Last Sunday. *Sagra del Tartufo,* Via Ripamonti, festival centered around truffles.

November: All cities. November 1, All Saints' Day, remembrance with flowers and *pane dei morti* (bread for the dead).

EATING OUT

Nearly everybody loves Italian food. Until a few years ago the foreigner's image of Italian cuisine was based solely upon Neapolitan, Sicilian and Calabrese dishes, since most Italian immigrants came from these regions. Lighter, more delicate northern cuisine has more recently made its way to our tables. It's usually tasty, simple, colourful and offered in multiple courses, including classics such as *risotto alla Milanese* and the famous *osso buco*.

WHERE TO EAT

Most major hotels offer English- or American-style **breakfast** buffets, often included in the room rate. If you are set on doing it Italian-style head for a little bar for your *prima colazione*. This is the time to order *cappuccino* sprinkled with powdered cocoa (upon request) to accompany your choice of a *brioche* ordered *vuoto* (empty), *con la marmalata* (with marmalade) or *la crema* (pastry cream). When ordering tea, you will be asked *al limone o latte* (with lemon or milk). The thick quasi-pudding-like *cioccolata calda* (hot chocolate) is almost a meal in itself.

Milan is the home of the *paninoteca* or sandwich bar. Due to the New York-paced lifestyle of the hardworking Milanese, there is little time for a three-hour Roman-style **lunch** here. *Panino Giusto* has several locations around the centre offering more sizable grilled and cold sandwiches than those offered in most bars. If you want a *primo* of pasta or risotto, or a salad, stop in a stand-up bar or a *tavola calda* where you can have a quick bite at the counter. Supplies for a picnic in the park or out in the country can be found at a *pizzicheria* (delicatessen).

For **dinner**, even if you're not overly budget conscious, bear in mind that the most elaborate *ristorante*, where prices match the opulence of the décor, is rarely the best value. In a relaxed *osteria*, a family-run *trattoria* or a Neapolitan-style *pizzeria*, which will serve much more than simply pizza, both the ambience and the food are just as enjoyable and your evening will generally have more character. In all cases, cover *(coperto)* and service *(servizio)* charges are usually included (even then, it's normal to leave something extra); if service is not included, leave about 10–15 percent for the waiter. Reservations are always recommended due to the unpredictable deluge of out-of-town diners in Milan for the frequent trade fairs. Sundays can also be tricky, as much of Milan (and most of its restaurants) tends to close down.

For more details, see the list of Recommended Restaurants starting on page 133.

WHAT TO EAT

Milan's ethnically mixed population makes for a wide variety of international cuisine available in an otherwise provincial kitchen. Here and throughout Lombardy, you'll find not only local specialties but those of other Italian regions as well. A fine selection of vegetarian restaurants have sprung up to satisfy the substantial increase of declared Italian vegetarians recently. But if you desire the

Feast your eyes – then feast – on endless cheese.

true native experience, stick to local specialties such as risotto, polenta and *osso buco* (stewed veal shank).

Antipasti

The average *trattoria* sets out a colorful display of its *antipasti* (appetizers) near the entrance to tantalize you. Get to know the delicacies on offer by creating your own assortment ***(antipasto misto)***. Attractive and tasty are room-temperature *peperoni* — green, yellow and red bell peppers grilled, skinned and marinated in olive oil and a little lemon juice. Grilled mushrooms (*funghi*), small squash *(zucchini)* and eggplant *(melanzane)* are served room-temperature, and artichokes *(carciofi)* and sliced fennel *(finocchio)* are also served raw, with a tangy dressing *(pinzimonio)*. One refreshing hors d'œuvre is the Neapolitan *mozzarella alla caprese*, slices of soft buffalo cheese and tomato with basil, olive oil and black pepper.

Try Sicilian tuna *(tonno)* with white beans and onions *(fagioli e cipolle)*. Mixed seafood appetizers ***(antipasto di mare)*** may include any of the following: scampi, prawns *(gamberi)*, mussels *(cozze)*, fresh sardines *(sarde)*, squid, *(calamari)* and octopus *(polpi)*.

Paper-thin ham from Parma or San Daniele is

Who knew salami could taste so good?

served with seasonal melon *(prosciutto con melone)* or fresh figs *(con fichi)* when in season. Most **salami** is mass-produced in Milan factories, but some restaurants do "import" farm-produced sausage from Emilia-Romagna, Tuscany or Liguria.

Primi (First Courses)

Although we are used to making a whole meal from a heaping plate of pasta, a more moderate portion here is considered a first dish, to be followed by a *secondo* (main course). The wait staff generally will not be offended though if you order a *primo* along with an appetizer and dessert.

The most popular **soups** are mixed vegetable *(minestrone)*. If you're feeling adventurous, go local and try *ris e ran,* a soup with rice and frogs legs. Brescia is famous for its soups with tortellini or rice, the latter much more savoury than its name *minestra sporca* or "dirty soup".

You'll usually run into the same few dozen variations, but it is said that there are as many different shapes of Italian **pasta** as there are Italian dialects, some 360 at last count, with new forms always being created. Each sauce – tomato, cheese, cream, meat or fish – is destined to a specific shape. In this land of artists, the pasta's shape and texture form an essential part of the taste, and pasta manufacturers commission noted designers to create new configurations. Besides spaghetti and macaroni, the worldwide popularity of pasta has familiarized us with *tagliatelle* (ribbon noodles), *lasagne* (layers of pasta laced with a meat and béchamel sauce), rolled *canelloni*, and *ravioli*. From there, you launch into the lusty poetry of *tortellini* and *fagotti* (variations on ravioli), or fat "tongues" of *linguine*, flat *pappardelle*, quill-shaped *penne* and the corrugated *rigatoni*. None will disappoint: try a different one at each meal.

Following the pasta profusion, there are almost as many **sauces**. A subtle variation on the ubiquitous tomato-based *bolognese* meat sauce is made with chopped chicken livers, white wine and celery. Others range from the simplest and spiciest *aglio, olio, pepperoncino* (garlic, olive oil, and hot peppers), *marinara* (tomato with oregano), *carbonara* (chopped bacon and eggs), *pesto* (basil and garlic ground up in olive oil with pine nuts and Parmesan cheese) and *vongole* (clams sometimes with a bit of tomato), to the succulent *lepre* (hare in red wine) and startling but wonderful *al nero* (pasta blackened by the ink of the cuttlefish). Parmesan is not automatically added to every pasta dish, and sauces using fish and mushroom are meant to be eaten without, so as to not overpower the delicate flavors. Follow your waiter's suggestion.

For Lombardy's princes and peasants alike, the Po valley paddies have made **risotto** a worthy rival to pasta. The rice has to be round and creamy, never long and dry. Northern tradition cooks it slowly in white wine, beef marrow, butter (not oil) and saffron, with Parmesan cheese melted in at the end of the cooking for the proper smooth finish. Delicious variations result when blended with seafood, chicken, mushrooms or whatever the daily market offers.

Secondi (Main Courses)

Veal *(vitello)* is Lombardy's main meat dish. The popular *cotoletta alla Milanese* (pounded veal cutlet) is known in some restaurants as the "elephant's ear" as they have pounded it so thin and wide. Brushed with egg, coated with breadcrumbs, and pan-fried in butter, it is not exactly a dietary dish, but when in Rome... For something a bit lighter, try *osso buco* (stewed veal shank), the *vitello tonnato* (veal in tuna sauce), or *alla fiorentina* (with spinach sauce).

The Roman *saltimbocca* ("jump in the mouth") frequents Lombardian menus with its veal rolled with ham and sage and cooked in Marsala wine. Calf's liver *(fegato)* is served *alla milanese* in breadcrumbs. Alternatively, it can be served *alla veneziana*, thinly sliced and sautéed with onions in olive oil.

Beef *(manzo)*, lamb *(agnello)*, pork *(maiale)* and chicken *(pollo)* are most often grilled or roasted *(al forno)*. Curious palates might like to tackle Milanese *busecca*, tripe with white beans, or *casoeula*, pork and sausages stewed in cabbage.

Although Milan is not a coastal city it does have a large **fish** market behind the Stazione Centrale. The best seafood meals are had, though, at restaurants that source directly from the nearby Ligurian shores and the freshwater lakes. Whole fish are prepared simply grilled, steamed, baked under a sea-salt crust or fried. Try the *spigola* (sea bass), *coda di rospa* (angler fish), *triglia* (red mullet) or even *pesce spada* (swordfish). *Fritto misto* usually means a mixed fry of fish, but can also include anything from chicken, calf's liver, veal and vegetables. Clarify with your waiter before you order.

Toni's Bread

Many great things were born of a mistake. The now-famous Milanese *panettone* was a quick recovery from a dessert gone wrong. Legend goes that it was Christmas Eve at the Castello Sforzesco under the reign of Ludovico, and the grand banquet was to finish with the court chef's secret-recipe dessert. After perhaps one *grappa* too many, the chef lost track of time and burned his creation. While he was fretting and desperate, Toni the dishwasher took the leftover dough of the original dessert, added candied fruit, spices, eggs, and sugar and popped it in the oven. When he took it out, it looked like a simple loaf of bread, but there was no alternative to offer. Dressed up on a silver tray and served in great style, it elicited perplexed reactions, but the final result was a success. Toni's bread *(pane di toni)* has evolved into today's plump panettone traditionally served during the Christmas season.

Cheeses and Dessert

Grana Padana is similar to Parmesan *(parmigiano)*, though the former is indigenous to this region. Besides grated over a *primo*, it is eaten by itself, and delicious with a drizzle of *aceto balsamico tradizionale* (balsamic vinegar). Try, too, the creamy blue *gorgonzola* from the nearby town of the same name, aromatic *bagoss* or a creamy chunk of aged *robiola*.

During the Easter and Christmas holidays look for the famous Milanese *colomba* or *panettone*, both egg-based leavened sweet breads studded with raisins. In some restaurants you will find local *torta di tagliatelle*, a dessert made from egg, almonds and cocoa. A more neutral finish to your meal is the Mantovan cornmeal-based *torta sbrisolona*.

Seasonal **fruit** is a lighter way to end the meal: grapes (*uva*), apples (*mele*) and tart blood oranges *(torchi)* in the autumn and winter; apricots *(albicocche)*, peaches *(pesche)* and wonderful fresh figs *(fichi)* in spring and summer.

Ice-cream comes in a wide variety of flavors and is generally much better in an ice-cream parlour *(gelateria)* than in most restaurants.

Wines

The wines from Lake Garda's east shores falling under the DOC zone of *Riviera del Garda* include *rosso* (red) and *chiaretto* (rosé). Other reds from the DOC zone of Oltrepò Pavese include *Barbacarlo*, *Barbera* and *Rosso*. The *Francacorta* DOC from the Brescia area includes reds, sparkling and still whites, as well as rosé.

You may also venture into the products of other regions such as Piedmont's splendid, full-bodied *Barolo*, a young Tuscan *Chianti Classico*, distinguished by the proud *gallo nero* (black rooster), a complex *Brunello* from further south in Tuscany or a dry white *Orvieto* from Umbria.

To help you digest your meal, try a *digestivo* of sweet *limoncello* from the south, or strong *grappa*; and for the more adventuresome an *amaro*, literally translated as "bitter."

To Help You Order ...

What do you recommend? **Cosa consiglia?**
Do you have a set menu? **Avete un menù a prezzo fisso?**
I'd like a/an/some... **Vorrei...**

beer	**una birra**	pepper	**del pepe**
bread	**del pane**	potatoes	**delle patate**
butter	**del burro**	salad	**dell'insalata**
coffee	**un caffè**	salt	**del sale**
fish	**del pesce**	soup	**una minestra**
fruit	**della frutta**	sugar	**dello zucchero**
ice cream	**un gelato**	tea	**un tè**
meat	**del carne**	water	**dell'acqua**
wine	**del vino**	milk	**del latte**

... and Read the Menu

aglio	garlic	**gamberi**	scampi, prawns
agnello	lamb	**mela**	apple
arancia	orange	**ostrica**	oyster
bistecca	beef steak	**pancetta**	bacon
carciofi	artichokes	**pesce**	fish
cipolle	onions	**piselli**	peas
coniglio	rabbit	**pollo**	chicken
costoletta	cutlet	**pomodoro**	tomato
cozze	mussels	**peperoni**	peppers
crostacei	shellfish	**pesca**	peach
fichi	figs	**uova**	eggs
formaggio	cheese	**vitello**	veal

HANDY TRAVEL TIPS

An A–Z Summary of Practical Information

A

ACCOMMODATION *(alloggio)*

(See also CAMPING, YOUTH HOSTELS and the list of RECOMMENDED HOTELS starting on page 125)

Hotels, called *hotel or alberghi*, are classified in categories ranging from five stars (luxury) down to one. Rates vary according to location, season, class and services, and are fixed in agreement with the regional tourist boards in Milan and in the lake district. Being an important business city, Milan's high- and low-season rates for hotels are determined mainly by frequent trade fairs and other commercial considerations outside the summer months, with several hotels in Milan even closing in August. At the lake resorts, where many hotels close after Christmas (or even before that, November to Easter), low season varies but usually runs from May through June and late-September through October.

Breakfast is usually included, and during high season at the lakes some resort hotels require guests to book a minimum of three nights half-board. Even if prices are listed as *tutto compreso* (inclusive of local taxes and service charges), check that the VAT sales tax (IVA) of 20% for five-star hotels and 10% for other categories is included.

It is advisable year round and essential in high season to book reservations in advance through travel agencies or by contacting the hotel directly; always get written confirmation. Once there, the APT (see TOURIST INFORMATION OFFICES) can supply local hotel lists. At Milan's Linate and Malpensa airports and the Stazione Centrale train station, information desks provide advice and booking facilities.

Hotel reservation service: Free services, Inphonline: Tel. 02/27201330 or (toll-free in Italy) (800)008777; fax 02/2564043; <www.initalia.it>, e-mail <info@initalia.it> and Centro

Prenotazioni Hotel Italia: Tel. 02/29531605; fax 02/29531586; <www.cphi.it>.

Pensione covers everything from a small, family-run hotel (breakfast included) to an elegant inn of a higher category. Those with shared baths are a dying breed, but can still be found.

Motels are increasing and improving in service. Many have swimming pools, tennis courts and other sports facilities. They are usually located right off the *autostrade*.

Self-catering accommodation. Families staying for a week or longer in one place may find it convenient and economical, especially in tourist resorts, to rent a furnished apartment or villa.

For further information contact: <www.italianvillas.com> or Agriturist, the National Association for Rural Tourism: Corso Vittorio Emanuele 101, 00186 Rome; Tel. 06/6852342; fax 06/6852424; <www.agriturist.it>.

I'd like a single/double room.	***Vorrei una camera singola/matromoniale.***
with bath/shower/private toilet	***con bagno/doccia/ gabinetto privato***

AIRPORTS (*aeroporti*)

Milan has two airports, **Malpensa**, 45 km (28 miles) northwest of the city centre for intercontinental traffic, and **Linate**, about 7 km (4 miles) to the east mainly for domestic and European flights. There is a bus service (Tel. 02/6690351) to Milan's central railway station, Stazione Centrale, about every 30 minutes from 6:05 am to 11:35 pm from Linate and every 20 minutes from 4:15 am to 12:15 am from Malpensa.

Malpensa and Linate Airport information: Tel. 02/7485220; <www.sea-aeroportmilano.it/Eng>. Lost baggage: Malpensa Tel. 02/58580069; Linate Tel. 02/70124451.

Bergamo has an airport at *Orio* (for domestic flights) 45 km (28 miles) from Milan; Tel. (035)326323.

B

BUDGETING FOR YOUR TRIP

Milan, a business-expense town, is considered to be fairly expensive in line with other major European cities. All prices are approximate, for guidance only.

Airport bus. To downtown Milan from Linate: €0.75–2.50, depending on the service; from Malpensa around €7.

Camping. €6 per person per night (children €2); car, caravan (trailer or camper) €8–12 per night; tent €6 per night; motorcycle free.

Car hire/rental. Booked on arrival in Milan, with unlimited mileage but collision/theft insurance and 20% tax extra: small (VW Polo) €80 per day, €380 per week; medium-range (Fiat Tipo) €120 per day, €550 per week.

Entertainment. Cinema €7; club (entrance and first drink) €10–20; opera €12–120.

Hotels. Double occupancy with private bathrooms per night, including service and taxes, no meals: inexpensive €50–85 moderate €85–180, luxury €180–600. (See also Recommended Hotels on page 125)

Meals and drinks. Continental breakfast €2–15; lunch or dinner in a good restaurant (including service but not wine) €20–40; bottle of wine, from €3; beer/soft drinks €1.50–4; apéritif €2.50–4; coffee served at a table €1.75–3.50, at the bar €0.75–2.

Museums. €1–8.

Public transport. Metro/bus/tram tickets €1 each; day-travel pass €3, two-day pass €5.50.

Shopping bag. 500g bread €0.75, 250g butter €1.75, 500g beefsteak €10–12.50, 200g coffee €2.50, bottle of wine €2.50+.

Taxis. Downtown Milan to Linate airport approximately €15–17.50; to Malpensa airport around €9; average trip in Milan €6–10.

Youth hostels. €13–15 per night, with breakfast.

C

CAMPING (*campeggio*)

You'll find plenty of campsites around the lakes and in the Milan area, notably the one at **Città di Milano**, Via Gaetano Airaghi, 61 (near Tangenziale Ovest motorway); Tel. 02/48200134; fax 02/48202999; call in advance to confirm dates. Alternatively, another Milan site is out at the **Autodromo di Monza**, Località Biassono; Tel. 039/387771; fax 039/320324; open from April to September. Addresses and details of amenities for the Lombardy region are given in the directory *Campeggi in Italia*, published by the Italian Touring Club (TCI), Corso Italia 10, 20122 Milan, Tel. 02/8526304 or 02/5359971; <www.touringclub.it/english>. A free list of sites, with location map, published by the Federcampeggio *(Federazione Italiana del Campeggio e del Caravanning)*, is available from the Italian National Tourist Office (see page 123) or from Federcampeggio: Via Vittorio Emanuele 11, 50041 Calenzano (Florence); Tel. 055/882 391.

Campsites at the lakes during the peak summer months of July and August are usually very crowded. Check with local tourist offices (see page 123) for information about reservations. Many campsites require guests to carry the *International Camping Carnet*, a pass that entitles holders to discounts and insurance coverage throughout Europe. The Carnet can be obtained through your camping or automobile association or from the TCI or Federcampeggio.

CAR RENTAL/HIRE (*autonoleggio*) (See also DRIVING)

Driving in Milan is taxing and not recommended to the uninitiated, so do all your sightseeing in the city, then rent a car for out-of-town excursions or to proceed to your next stop.

The best rates are usually found by booking directly with an international rental company and paying for your car before you leave home, or as part of a "fly-drive" package. Check that the quoted rate includes Collision Damage Waiver, unlimited mileage, tax, and if the car has to be returned to its starting point (eg, clarify an airport vs. downtown location as they may result in different rates), as these can greatly increase the cost.

You will need a driver's licence (EU model for EU citizens) for at least 12 months, shown at the time of rental. You will also need to show your passport and a major credit card. Minimum age is 21 or 25 depending on the company and the car's engine size. Gasoline *(benzina)* is priced per litre (4 liters per gallon) and can cost about €1.

CLIMATE (*clima*)

In the Po Valley, summers are very hot and humid, while winters are cold and foggy. Temperatures are at their most extreme in and directly around Milan itself; the lake regions are generally a couple of degrees cooler. The best time to visit Milan is in spring or autumn between April and June or in September. As the luxuriant vegetation testifies, winters around the lakes can offer surprisingly mild days, but can also be as bitingly cold.

		J	F	M	A	M	J	J	A	S	O	N	D
F°	max	40	46	56	65	74	80	84	85	75	63	51	43
	min	32	35	43	49	57	63	67	66	61	52	43	35
C°	max	5	8	13	18	23	27	29	29	24	17	10	6
	min	0	2	6	10	14	17	19	19	16	11	6	2

CLOTHING

Apart from June, July and August, in the city or out at the lakes, pack a sweater for the evenings. You'll need rainwear in spring and autumn, boots and overcoat in the winter. Good walking shoes are essential all year round. Remember that churches are places of worship as well as works of art and architecture, and visitors should dress respectably.

COMPLAINTS *(reclami)*

To avoid problems, always establish prices in advance, such as when dealing with porters at stations. For complaints about taxi fares, refer to a notice, in four languages, affixed by law in each taxi, specifying extra charges (airport runs, Sunday or holiday rates, night or baggage surcharge) in excess of the meter rate.

CRIME AND SAFETY

Cases of violence against tourists are rare, but petty theft is an endless annoyance; tourists are always easy targets for robbery.

Check whether your home insurance policy covers theft or loss of personal effects while abroad; if it does not, it is advisable to take out separate insurance.

Take usual precautions against theft – don't carry large amounts of cash, leave your valuables in the hotel safe, not in your room. The main danger is from pickpockets, especially in busy markets and on buses. Beware of gypsy girls with babies or young children – while they distract your attention begging for coins, an accomplice may be behind you dipping into any available pockets and bags. Make photocopies of your tickets, driving licence, passport and other vital documents to facilitate reporting a theft and obtaining replacements. Better to be safe than sorry.

Any theft or loss must be reported immediately to the police and you should obtain a copy of the report in order to comply with your travel insurance. If your passport is lost or stolen, you should also inform your consulate or embassy.

My wallet/passport/ticket has been stolen.	***Mi hanno rubato il portafoglio/il passaporto/il biglietto.***

CUSTOMS (*dogana*) AND ENTRY REQUIREMENTS

For citizens of EU countries, a valid passport or identity card is all that is needed to enter Italy for up to 90 days. Citizens of Australia, New Zealand and the US also need only a valid passport.

Visas *(permesso di soggiorno).* For stays of more than 90 days a special visa or residence permit is required. For full information on passport and visa regulations check with the Italian Embassy in your country.

Free exchange of non-duty-free goods – for personal use only – is allowed between EU countries. Refer to your home country's regulating organization for a current and complete list of import restrictions.

Currency restrictions. Tourists may bring an unlimited amount of Italian or foreign currency into the country. On departure, however, you must declare any currency beyond the equivalent of €10,000, so it's wise to declare sums exceeding this amount when you arrive.

I've nothing to declare.	***Non ho niente da dichiarare.***

D

DRIVING

Motorists planning to take their vehicle into Italy need a full driver's licence accompanied by a translation (available from your local automobile association), an International Motor Insurance Certificate and a Vehicle Registration Document. Drivers entering Italy in a private car registered to another person must have the owner's written permission, translated. A green insurance card is not a legal requirement, but it is strongly recommended for travel within Italy. Foreign visitors must display an official nationality sticker, and, if coming from the UK or Ireland, headlights must be adjusted for driving on the right. Full details are available from your automobile association, or from your insurance company.

The use of seat belts in front and back seats is obligatory; fines for non-compliance are stiff. A red warning triangle must be carried in case of breakdown. Motorcycle riders must wear crash helmets. The A.C.I.

(Automobile club d'Italia; <www.aci.it/English>) gives information on-line worth consulting before your departure.

In Milan, the ban on private cars is taking hold and being enforced. And parking can be impossible and costly.

Driving conditions. Drive on the right, pass on the left. Give way to traffic coming from the right. Speed limits: 50 km/h (30 mph) in town, 90 km/h (55 mph) on freeways, and 130 km/h (80 mph) on highways. The freeways (*superstrada*, indicated with blue signs) and most highways (*autostrada*, indicated with green signs) are excellent, skillfully designed for fast driving. Italian autostradas are toll roads – you take an entry ticket and pay at the other end for the distance travelled. Be careful not to enter exclusive "TelePass" (automatic toll meter) lanes; otherwise you will be constricted to back up and incur a fine.

Rules and Regulations. Italian traffic police *(polizia stradale)* are authorized to impose on-the-spot fines for speeding and other traffic offences, such as driving while intoxicated or stopping in a no-stopping zone. Police have become stricter about speeding, and are beginning to install hidden speed regulators with cameras. Don't be fooled: rental cars and their drivers are easily tracked down even once the cars have been returned.

Fuel *(benzina).* Petrol (gasoline) is sold at three grades. The grades available are Super (98–100 octane), Normal (86 – 88 octane) and Senza Piombo (unleaded). Petrol stations are generally open 7am–12:30pm and 3–7:30pm. Many are self-service assessible by an automatic payment machine that accepts credit cards and Italian currency (bills). Most stations along the highway are attended 24 hours a day. Be aware that a station marked "Gas" indicates that it has methane gas and may not offer unleaded petrol in addition.

Parking (*posteggio/parcheggio*) in Milan is highly restricted. In areas open to non-residents, a pre-paid *Sostamilano* Card, available from authorized retailers and uniformed A.T.M. (*Azienda Transporti Municipali*) personnel, is required to be displayed on the dashboard or rearview mirror. The A.T.M. operates free parking lots outside the city (the city centre is easily reached by public transport); Tel. (toll-free in Italy) (800)016857.

If You Need Help. Should you be involved in a road accident, contact the Carabinieri. About every 2 km (1½ miles) on the autostrada there's an emergency call box marked "SOS". If you require a tow truck call 116 for assistance, but be aware that you will be charged; be sure that you have breakdown insurance coverage before you leave home. If your car has been towed, contact the *Comando Centrale Polizia Municipale*, Piazza Beccaria, Tel. 02/77271. If your car has been stolen or broken into contact the local Urban Police Headquarters (Questura) and get a copy of their report for your insurance claim.

Road signs. Road signs in Italy are international.

(International) Driving License	***patente (internazionale)***
car registration papers	***libretto di circolazione***
Fill the tank please.	***Per favore, faccia il pieno.***
There's been an accident.	***C'è stato un incidente.***

E

ELECTRICITY

220V/50Hz AC is standard. An adapter for continental-style sockets will be needed; American 110V appliances also require a transformer. It is easy to obtain one before leaving home.

an adaptor plug	***una presa complementare***
a voltage transformer	***un trasformatore***

EMBASSIES and CONSULATES (*ambasciata; consulato*)

Embassies are located in Rome but each country has a Consulate office in Milan. Most offices are only open from 9am to 12pm so give a call before you drop by. We have listed some websites for a number of Rome Embassies as well.

Australia: Via Borgogna 2; Tel. 02/7772941; fax 02/77704242; <www.australian-embassy.it/>.
Canada: Via Vittor Pisani 19; Tel. 02/67581; <www.canada.it>.
New Zealand: Via G. D'Arezzo 6; Tel. 02/48012544; fax 02/48012577; e-mail <nzemb.rom@flashnet.it>.
Republic of Ireland: Piazza S. Pietro in Gessate; Tel. 02/55187569; fax 02/55187570.
South Africa: Vicolo S. Giovanni sul Muro 4; Tel. 02/809036; fax 02/72011063.
UK: Via San Paolo 7; Tel. 02/723001; fax 02/86465081.
US: Via Principe Amedeo 2/10; Tel. 02/290351; fax 02/29001165; <www.usis.it/>.

EMERGENCIES (See also POLICE and HEALTH AND MEDICAL CARE)
The following numbers are in operation 24 hours a day. If you don't speak Italian, it's best to find a local resident to help you, or speak to the English-speaking operator on the telephone assisted service, Tel. 170.

Police	112
General Emergency	113
Fire	115
Paramedics	118

Please, can you place an emergency call to the...	***Per favore, può fare una telefonata d'emergenza...***
police	***alla polizia***
fire department	***ai vigili del fuoco***
hospital	***all'ospedale***

G

GAY AND LESBIAN TRAVELERS

Milan is arguably Italy's most gay-friendly city, with an interesting international community of men and women working in fields of fashion, design and publishing. ARCI-gay, the national gay rights organization is a great source for finding gay-friendly localities. Contact Arcigay-Milano; Via Evangelista Torricelli, 19 20136 Milano; Tel. 02/58100399; help line 02/89401749; fax 02/8394604.

GETTING THERE

By Air

Scheduled flights. Most transatlantic flights direct to Milan come into Malpensa, with European and domestic flights arriving at Linate (see AIRPORTS on page 102). Look for special deals especially during off-season months when commercial flights are never sold out. Be careful about the precise conditions of booking and travel and ask all the right questions. If you are considering going elsewhere in Italy, ask if you can fly into Milan and then out of say, Rome.

Package tours can be booked or created with local travel agents or at the Compagnia Italian Turismo (CIT see below, under By Rail), Italy's national travel agency and tour operator.

By Road (see also DRIVING)

The road system within Italy is very manageable from north to south (including ferry transport connections to Sicily and Sardinia) and accessible when arriving from France, Switzerland and Austria.

By Rail

Ferrovie dello Stato (FS), Italian State Railways offices (Tel. 051/257911 or (848)888088 (toll-free in Italy); <www.fs-on-line.com>) will help tourists traveling by rail to plan an itinerary. Ask about special discounts for students, families and senior citizens. If you plan on travelling to other cities as well, ask about Euro-Rail and Kilometric tickets:

Australia, CIT, Level 2, 263 Clarence Street, Sydney; Tel. (612)92671255.

Canada, CIT World Travel Group, 1450 City Councillors, Suite 750, Montreal, Que. H3A IV4, Tel. (541)8464310800; Alba Tours Canada Leisure Group, 130 Merton Street, Toronto, Ont. M5R 3J8; Tel. (416)7462890.

South Africa, World Travel Agency, 8th Floor, Everite House 20, De Korte Street Braamfontein, Johannesburg.

UK, Rail Choice Delta House, 175-177 Borough High Street, London, SE1 1XP; Tel. (020)79399915; fax (020)79399916.

US, 342 Madison Avenue, Suite 207, New York, NY 10173, Tel. toll-free (800)248-7245.

Travellers from countries where the FS is not represented should contact an international travel agency.

Be aware of the infamous Italian *sciopero* or train strikes that can last from a few hours to a few days. They are less frequent and less lengthy than those of years ago, and are publicized in the newspapers at least one day in advance.

When's the next bus/ train to ...?	***Quando parte il prossimo autobus/treno per...?***
single (one-way)/ return (round-trip)	***andata/ andata e ritorno***
first/second class	***prima/seconda classe***

GUIDES AND TOURS

Many of Milan's and the lake area's larger hotels can make arrangements for multilingual guides or interpreters to accompany groups as well as individuals. A tour-guide service for Milan operates from the city tourist office (see page 123), APT, Via Marconi 1 (Metro: Duomo); Tel. and fax 02/72524300. A three-hour bus tour of Milan with *Agenzia Auostradale, Tel. 02/801161* departs from the Duomo, alongside the APT center (Tuesday to Sunday at 9:30am; around €35). On Mondays, instead, a walking tour of the city centre is offered from the same departure point. (10am; approximately €15).

H

HEALTH AND MEDICAL CARE

If your health-insurance policy does not cover you while abroad, take out a short-term policy with your insurance company, or travel agency before leaving home. EU citizens are entitled to free emergency hospital treatment if they have form E111 (obtainable from a post office before leaving home). Keep receipts so that you can claim a refund when you return home.

If you need medical care, ask your hotel receptionist or local consulate or Embassy to find a doctor (or dentist) who speaks English. Milan's *Servizio di Pronto Soccorso* (Emergency Room) functions day and night at the Policlinico hospital, Via Francesco Sforza 35 (Metro: Crocetta); Tel. 02/ 55031.

Throughout Italy, in an emergency you can telephone 118 to call for an ambulance.

Pharmacies. The *farmacia* is open during shopping hours (see Opening Hours), and an all-night service is also available at Stazione Centrale; Tel. 02/6690935. No vaccinations are required for entry into Italy. Bring along an adequate supply of any prescribed medication.

I need a doctor/dentist.	***Ho bisogno di un medico/dentista.***
It hurts here.	***Ho un dolore qui.***

HOLIDAYS (*festa*)

When a national holiday falls on a Friday or a Monday, Italians may make a *ponte* (bridge) or long weekend. Banks, government offices, shops, museums and galleries are typically closed on the following days:

January 1	*Capodanno or Primo dell'Anno*	New Year's Day
January 6	*Epifania*	Epiphany
April 25	*Festa della Liberazione*	Liberation Day
May 1	*Festa del Lavoro*	Labour Day
August 15	*Ferragosto*	Assumption Day
November 1	*Ognissanti*	All Saint's Day
December 7	*Sant'Ambrogio*	Milan's Patron Saint Ambrose
December 8	*L'Immacolata Concezione*	Immaculate Conception
December 25	*Natale*	Christmas Day
December 26	*Santo Stefano*	St Stephen's Day
Movable dates:	*Pasqua*	Easter
	Lunedì di Pasqua	Easter Monday

L

LANGUAGE

Staff at the major hotels and shops of Milan and the resorts usually speaks some English. Most Italians appreciate foreigners trying to communicate in their language.

LAUNDRY AND DRY CLEANING (*lavanderia, tintoria*)

There are now coin-operated, self-service laundromats all over the Milan area; ask your concierge where the closest one is located. Next-day full service is furnished by a *tintoria* or *lavanderia.* Specify if you would like your items washed and ironed (*lavata e stirata*) or dry-cleaned (*lava a secco*). Such services are commonly more economical though less convenient than the in-house service offered by hotels.

M

MEDIA

Newspapers and magazines (*giornale; rivista*). You can find newspapers in English at airports and in city-centre newsstands *(edicola)*: *Wall Street Journal Europe*, *The International Herald Tribune*. Listings of current happenings, easily decipherable in the Italian publications are: *Viva Milano,* a special insert published in Wednesday's Edition of Milan's daily *Corriere della Sera* or *Tutto Milano* a special insert, in the Rome-based *La Repubblica* on Thursdays. This sports-mad country also has a daily paper, *La Gazetta dello Sport*, devoted to events not only in Italy but all over the world.

Radio and TV *(radio, televisione)*. The Italian state TV network, the RAI (Radio Televisione Italiana), broadcasts three TV channels, which compete with six independent channels. Most of the better hotels and rental properties have cable connections which show CNN Europe and CNBC all day, offering world news broadcast in English. The airwaves are crammed with radio stations, most of them broadcasting popular music. The BBC World Service can be picked up on 1209.5 AM in the morning and 733KHz AM in the evenings.

MONEY MATTERS

Currency (*soldi*). Italy's monetary unit is the *Euro* (abbreviated to €), which is divided into 100 *cents*. Banknotes are available in denominations of 500, 200, 100, 50, 20, 10 and 5 Euros. There are coins for 2 and 1 Euro, and for 50, 20, 10, 5, 2 and 1 cent. For information on currency restrictions when travelling to and from Italy, see CUSTOMS AND ENTRY REGULATIONS.

Banks and currency exchange. (See also OPENING HOURS). Money can be changed at currency-exchange offices *(ufficio di cambio)* in main railway stations and airports and in tourist-frequented areas in the centre of the city. However, the exchange rate at these offices tends to be less advantageous than that offered by banks (be sure to check the small print for commission per each exchange). The same applies to foreign currency or traveller's checks changed in hotels, shops or restaurants. Taking cash advances from ATMS (*bank-o-mat*) on your credit card usually offers the best exchange rate, but first check with your bank at home to make sure that your account is authorized for international withdrawals with a PIN number that works overseas.

Credit cards, debit cards and travellers' cheques. Most hotels, many shops, service stations and restaurants honour major international credit cards. Travellers' cheques are widely accepted in most cities and tourist resorts. Outside main towns, it's best to always have some cash handy. Remember to take your passport or national identity card when you go to cash a cheque.

Can I pay with this credit card?	***Posso pagare con la carta di credito?***
Where is an ATM?	***Dov'è il bancomat?***

O

OPENING HOURS (*orari di apertura*)

Banks are generally open 8am–1:30pm and 2:30–4pm, Monday to Friday. Currency exchange offices at airports and major railway stations are open till late in the evening and on Saturdays and Sundays and sometimes during lunch hours.

Churches generally close for sightseeing at lunchtime, approximately noon to 3pm or even later, and discourage tourist visits during Sunday morning services.

Museums and art galleries are usually open from 9 or 9:30am to

2, 3 or 4pm, and in some cases from 5–8pm, Tuesday to Saturday, and until 1pm on Sundays. Closing day is generally Monday. Pick up a schedule from the Tourist Information Office (see page 123) for ever-changing exceptions.

Post offices normally open Monday-Friday 8:05 or 8:30am–2 or 2:30pm; until noon on Saturday.

Shops in Milan are closed for a half-day Monday morning; food shops for a half-day Monday afternoon. All are open Tuesday–Saturday 9am–noon, 3:30–7:30pm. Some of the larger shops have open hours on Sundays. Shops in tourist resorts may even stay open all day, every day, in high season. Not all stores may stay open during the month of August whether in town or in resort areas.

P

POLICE (See also Crime and Safety and Emergencies)

The municipal police *(vigili urbani)* direct traffic and handle routine tasks, sometimes acting as unoffical interpreters. Look for the special badge on their uniforms. The *Carabinieri*, a paramilitary force, deal with violent or serious crimes and demonstrations. Their headquarters, the *Questura*, deals with visas and other complaints, and is a good point of reference if you need help from the authorities. Outside town, the Polizia Stradale patrol the highways, issue speeding tickets, and assist with breakdowns (see also Driving). In an emergency, dial 112 or 113 for police assistance.

POST OFFICES *(posta or ufficio postale)* (See Opening Hours)

Post offices, identified by the "PT" sign, handle telegrams, faxes, mail and money transfers. The main post office at Piazza Cordusio 1 (Metro: Cordusio) offers normal mailing facilities and services weekdays 8am–7pm.

Postage stamps can also be purchased at tobacconists and at some hotels. Note that *Posta Prioritaria* is a new service that costs a little more than standard post but is much faster.

Letterboxes are painted red; the slot marked "Per la Città" is for local mail, while the one labelled "Altre Destinazioni" is for all other destinations. The blue box is for expedited international post.

PUBLIC TRANSPORTATION (*trasporto publico*)

Taxis ***(tassì).*** Your best chance of finding a taxi during busy hours is ordering one by phone. Otherwise ask for the nearest taxi rank, usually found directly in or near all major piazzas. Make sure that the meter is running. Extra charges for luggage and for trips at night, on holidays, and to airports are posted inside every cab. It is normal practice to round up the fare. Beware of non-metered, unlicenced taxis. Radio-Taxi in Milan: Tel. 02/6767, 02/8383, or 02/8585.

Underground/Subway ***(Metrò).*** Milan has three major underground lines coded red (M1), green (M2) and yellow (M3), serving all the major tourist sights. A bright red "M" sign marks the station entrances. Tickets are available at newsstands, tobacconists and Metro stations, and trains run roughly from 6am to just after midnight.

Buses/trams ***(autobus/tram)*** require the same tickets as the metro. They are valid for a comprehensive 75 minutes so if you continue a trip from the Metro to a bus, remember to time stamp it again on board, or you will risk a stiff fine. The network of bus and tram lines is slightly complicated; look at the scheduled stop sign for your destination before boarding. A map of both networks is available from the tourist information office (see page 123), other details from the A.T.M. (Azienda Trasporti Milanesi; Tel. 02/745-2015; <www.atm-mi.it>), the well-organized information office in the Duomo Metro station right under the main Tourist Information Office.

Trains. The Italian State Railway (Ferrovie dello Stato; Tel. 02/63711; <www.fs-on-line.com>) offers a service with moderate fares. The green M2 Metro line serves all of Milan's railway stations. Journey times, depend on the type of train. Be aware of the infamous Italian sciopero or transportation strikes regarding all methods of public transportation. Check with your hotel before setting out for the day. Always remember to punch (thus validating) all tickets before boarding the train; automatic machines are found at the foot of each platform.

Italian trains are classified according to speed. Best and fastest are the Eurostar (first and second class; requiring supplementary fare and seat reservations), which have their own ticketing windows at all stations. Other classifications are Intercity (IC; first and second class; requiring supplementary fare and seat reservations) and the Espresso (E; first and second class; require supplementary fare and seat reservations). The Diretto (D) makes a number of local stops. There are two slower local trains, the InterRegionale (IR; first and second class) and Regionale (REG; second class only). Tickets can be purchased and reservations made at a local travel agency or at the railway station (allow for time).

Ferries/Lake Cruises. Each of the three lakes has a fleet of rapid hydrofoils and more leisurely ferries. Every lake has a paddle steamer dating from the early 1900's. The most luxurious of the modern boats is the Verbania on Lake Maggiore, carrying up to 1,000 passengers with a 360-seat restaurant.

Tickets can be purchased at any stop on the lakes. During the warm season, there are open ticket options that allow you to either travel between two points an unlimited number of times, or which allow you to get on and off at any stop; both for a determined time period.

Milano. Information and timetables only for travel on the lakes can be found at: Navigazione Lago Maggiore, Garda e di Como, Via Lodovico Ariosto 21 (Metro Conciliazione); Tel. 02/4676101; fax 02/46761059; <www.navigazionelagi.it>.

Lake Como. For timetables about lake cruises contact Navigazione Lago di Como, Via per Cernobbio 18; Tel. 031/579211; fax 031/570080. The main towns served by boat and hydrofoil are Como, Tremezzo, Bellagio, Menaggio, and (on west shore) Varenna and Bellano. A car ferry links Bellagio, Cadenabbia, Varenna and Menaggio.

Lake Garda. Cruise from Desenzano all the way north to Riva del Garda in just over four hours. Contact Navigazione Lago di Garda, Piazza Matteotti 2, Desenzano sul Garda; Tel. 030/9149511; fax 030/9149520.

Lake Maggiore. Cruise anywhere between Arona at the southern end and over the Swiss border all the way to Locarno. Stops include Stresa, Baveno, Pallanza, Intra, and Laveno and the lake's 3 islands. For details in advance, contact Navigazione Lago Maggiore, Viale F Baracca 1, Arona; Tel. 0322/233200; fax 0322/249530.

R

RELIGION

Roman Catholic mass is celebrated daily (several times on Sunday) in Italian. On Sundays, services in English are held at S. Maria del Carmine at 10 a.m. and 4:30 p.m.; Piazza del Carmine; Tel. 02/864-633-65. Information about Protestant services may be obtained from Cristiana Protestante (Luterana e Svizzera), at Via M. de Marchi 9; tel. 02/6552858.

Jewish Sabbath and holy days are celebrated in the dually Sephardic and Ashkenazi Synagogue on Via Guastalla in the Duomo area; Tel. 02/5512029.

For Moslems, there is the Moschea Al-Rahmàn; Via Cassanese 3/5 Segrate; Tel. 02/269-215-33.

What time is mass?	**A che ora è la messa?**
the service?	**la funzione?**

T

TELEPHONES (*telefono*)

You can make local and international calls from the orange public telephones located around town. In SIP (Societá Italiana per l'Esercizio

Telefonico) offices, you can also make long-distance and international calls; they are usually open from 7 am to around 10 pm. Some payphones accept coins and phone-cards *(scheda telefonica)* , while others accept phone-cards only; cards of various amounts can be bought from tobacconists. To make an international call, dial 00, followed by the country code (UK +44, US & Canada +1, New Zealand +64, Australia +61, South Africa +27, Ireland +353, Malta +356), then the area code (often minus the initial zero), and finally the number you are trying to reach.

If you use your calling card, the following are a list of access numbers for your country's toll free centres. (N.B. You must always insert a coin or a card to access a line even when making a toll free call. Be aware of the possibility of exorbitant hotel charges; check at the front desk before calling.)

Remember that as of recently you must always use the city prefix even when calling within the city and between Italian cities as well. For example dial (02) when calling from within Milan.

US	AT&T 1721011, Sprint 1721877, MCI 1721022, Bell Atlantic 1721010	
Canada	AT&T 1721002	Teleglobe 1721001
Australia	Optus 1721161	Telstra 1721061
New Zeland	1721064	
Ireland	1720353	
Malta	1720356	
UK	BT 1720044, Automatic 1720144, Mercury 1720544	

To place collect or operator-assisted calls use the following numbers:

numbers:	In Italy	1795
	International	170 (for English-speaking operators)
For directory assistance:	In Italy	12
	International	176 (for English-speaking operators)

Fax (transmission only) is available at the main Cordusio post office (see above) and at the Stazione Centrale office, open everyday 8am–9:30pm. Almost all hotels offer this service, as do a number of office supply or stationary stores around town.

Give me coins/a telephone card, please.	***Per favore, mi dia monette/una scheda telefonica.***

TIME ZONES

Italy follows Central European Time (GMT + 1). From the last Sunday in March to the last Sunday in October, clocks are put ahead one hour.

Vancouver	NewYork	London	**Rome**	Johannesburg	Sydney	Auckland
3 am	6 am	11 am	**noon**	1 pm	8 pm	10 pm

What time is it? ***Che ore sono?***

TIPPING

A service charge of approximately 15% is added to hotel and restaurant bills. If prices are quoted as all-inclusive, *tutto compreso*, the service charge is included, but not necessarily the IVA (VAT/sales tax, 20%); ask if you're not sure. In restaurants, in addition to the service charge, it is customary to give the waiter something extra. Bellboys, doormen, bartenders, and service-station attendants all expect a tip.

Thank you, this is for you.	***Grazie, questo è per lei.***

TOILETS

Toilets may be labelled with a symbol of a man or a woman or the initials W.C. (water closet) or: Uomini (men), Donne (women). Equally, Signori with an *i* is for men, Signore with an *e* is for women. Toilets in the Train Station and Metro stops may require a coin payment to enter. If you use a bar or café's bathroom, you are expected to buy something.

Where are the toilets?	***Dove sono i gabinetti?***

TOURIST INFORMATION OFFICES

The Italian National Tourist Office (ENIT, Ente Nazionale Italiano per il Turismo; central office: Via Marghera 2/6 00185 Roma; Tel. 06/49711; fax 06/4463379 or 06/4469907; <www.enit.it/>; e-mail <sedecentrale.enit@interbusiness.it) publishes detailed brochures with relatively up-to-date information on Milan, Lombardy, and the lakes. They cover transport and accommodation (including campsites). The Italian National Tourist Office can be found abroad in the following locations:

Australia and New Zealand, 44 Market Street NSW 2000 Sydney; Tel. (61)292-621666; fax (61)292 B 621677; e-mail <enitour@ihug.com.au>.

Canada, 17 Bloor Street East Suite 907, South Tower, M4W3R8 Toronto (Ontario); Tel. (1)4169254882/9253725; fax (1)4169254799; <www.italiantourism.com>; e-mail <enit.canada@on.aibn.com>

Republic of Ireland, 47 Merrion Square, Dublin 2; Tel. (01) 766-397

South Africa, London House, 21 Loveday Street, P.O. Box 6507, Johannesburg 2000; Tel. (11) 838-3247

UK,1 Princes Street, London W1R 88AY; Tel. (20)73551557/73551439; fax (20)74936695; e-mail <Enitlond@globalnet.co.uk>.

US, 500 North Michigan Avenue, Suite 401, Chicago, IL 60611; Tel. (312)6440990,6; fax (312)6443019; e-mail <enitch@italiantourism.com>.

Locally, you will find municipal or regional offices (APT, Azienda di Promozione Turistica) in Milan and all the major resort towns. These can be helpful with information (but not reservations) for last-minute accommodation needs.

Bergamo: A.P.T.; Via Vittorio Emanuele 20; 24121 Bergamo; Tel. 035/213185; fax 035/230184.

Como: Piazza Cavour 17; Tel. 031/269712; fax 031/240111; <www.lakecomo.com>
Milan: Via Marconi 1, 20123 Milan (Metro: Duomo); Tel. 02/72524301/2/3, fax 02/72524350; Stazione Centrale: Galleria di Testa; Tel./fax 02/72524360/70.
Monza:Piazza Carducci; Tel./fax039/323222 <www.monza.net/promonza>.
Stresa: Via Canonica 8; Tel. 0323/30150, fax 0323/32561. <www.laggiomagiorre.it>

W

WEIGHTS AND MEASURES

Italy uses the metric system.

Y

YOUTH HOSTELS (*ostello della Gioventù*)

Milan's hostel west of the city centre is near the San Siro race-course; AIG Ostello Rotta, Via Salmoiraghi 1, 20100 MI; Tel./fax 02/39267095. (Take number 1 Metro Red Line to QT8) It is open to holders of membership cards issued by the International Youth Hostels Federation. Book well in advance. La Cordata (Casa Scout) is a privately-run hostel on Via Burigozzo, 11, 20100 MI; Tel. 02/58314675 (Take the number 3 Metro yellow line to Missori). Cards and information are available from your national youth hostels association and from the Associazione Italiana Alberghi per la Gioventù (AIG), the Italian Youth Hostels Association, at: Via Cavour 44, 00184 Rome; Tel. 06/4871152; fax 06/4880492; <www.hostles-aig.org/shop-it/it-map.htm>; e-mail <aig@uni.net>.

Recommended Hotels

The Italian government rates hotels from one star to "five star L"(luxury). These ratings are based solely on amenities provided – not on appearances or quality of service. Prices almost always include some type of breakfast, but double-check when booking. Below you will find a range of lodgings throughout Milan and the Lake district; always book ahead and have your faxed confirmation in hand when checking in. You will always need to leave your passport with the desk when registering, according to Italian law. It will be returned to you later. Rates vary widely depending on seasons and trade fairs in Milan; Milan's city hotels are always priced higher than the surrounding areas. All listed hotels accept major credit cards, and are wheelchair accessible unless otherwise indicated. Hotels in the lake area stay open year round, unless noted otherwise.

The price ranges below indicate a double occupancy room with bath or shower, including service and IVA (sales taxes) in high season. These ranges should be used as guides only.

€	below €75
€€	€75–150
€€€	€150–250
€€€€	€250 and above

MILAN

Antica Locanda Leonardo €€ *Corso Magenta 78; Tel. 02/463317; fax 02/48019012; <www.leoloc.com>*. Set back in a quiet courtyard down the street from Leonardo da Vinci's *Last Supper*, this recently renovated pensione-like hotel is tastefully decorated and welcomes guests as if they were family. Closed five days over Christmas and three weeks in August. 20 rooms.

Arno € *Via Lazzaretto 17; Tel./fax 02/6705509; email <hotelarno@libero.it>*. Very friendly hotel conveniently located near the train station. Free internet access and use of kitchen facilities. 9–14 rooms.

Carrobbio €€ *Via Medici 3; Tel. 02/89010740; fax 02/8053334; email <hotel_carrobio@traveleurope.it>*. A short distance to the Duomo in a shopping area close to cafés and an up-and-coming artsy neighborhood. Closed August and Christmas. 53 rooms.

De la Ville €€€€ *Via Hoepli 6; Tel. 02/867651; fax 02/866609; email <dlvbook@tin.it>*. Great for the Duomo, opera, and shopping. Elegant interiors, bar, full gym and sauna. 108 rooms.

Excelsior Gallia €€€€ *Piazza Duca d'Aosta 9; Tel. 02/67851; fax 02/66713239; <www.excelciorgallia.it>*. Situated next to the main station, this grand institution offers all of the commodities a client could desire from his/her own personal concierge. Ultra lush décor with a lot of gold trim and red velvet. 250 rooms.

Four Seasons €€€€ *Via Gesù 8; Tel. 02/77088, fax 02/77085000; email <milano@fourseasons.com>*. Five-star luxury hotel with top-drawer attention to service and a light contemporary feel despite its location in a centuries-old ex-convent. Two popular in-house restaurants and private parking all located within steps of the Via Montenapoleone shopping district. 118 rooms.

Grand Hotel Brun €€€ *Via Caldera 21; Tel. 02/45271, fax 02/ 48204746; email <brunrest@tin.it>*. Tranquil location out of the bustle of the centre; convenient for any trade fair (and the soccer stadium). Private parking available. 324 rooms.

Grand Hotel Duomo €€€€ *Via San Raffaele 1; Tel. 02/8833,fax02/86462027;<www.grandhotelduomo.com>*.

A convenient classic, right on the cathedral square with a spectacular roof-terrace. Discreet and friendly service happy to accommodate the large numbers of return business guests. 158 rooms.

London €€ *Via Rovello 3; Tel. 02/72020166, fax 02/8057037.* Simple and clean and centrally located right near the Castello Sforzesco. Air-conditioned in the summer and heated well in the winter. Clarify with or without showers when booking rooms. Closed August and Christmas; 33 rooms.

Manin €€-€€€ *Via Manin 7; Tel. 02/6596511; fax 02/6552160;<www.hotel-manin.it>.* Friendly, standard hotel overlooking the public gardens. Close enough to all sights to make this a bargain. Closed 3 weeks in August. 118 rooms.

Michelangelo €€€ *Via Scarlatti 33; Tel 02/67551; fax 02/6694232; email<michelangelo@milanhotel.it>.* Popular with groups and conventions, and conveniently located next to main station, this hotel offers functional comfort with a smile. Parking and non-smoking rooms available. 306 rooms.

Palace €€€€ *Piazza della Repubblica 20; Tel. 02/63361;fax02/654485;email<westinpalacemilan@ westin.com>.* A prime example of imperial Napoleonic luxury in décor and service. One of the busiest hotels with a constant flow of international expense-account patrons through their rotating doors. Closed August. 244 rooms.

Pensione Argentario € *Corsa Porta Vittoria 58; Tel. 02/5464532; fax 02/5464532.* Location is quite central; impeccably clean, with friendly service. At these prices, expect showers to be separate and no television. 25 rooms.

Pierre €€€ *Via Edmondo de Amicis 32; Tel. 02/72000581; fax 02/8052157; <www.hotelpierre.it>.* Ultra modern hotel with details such as telephones in the bathroom and remote control window shades. Very international clientele and friendly can-do service, located right near the Duomo. 51 rooms.

Principe di Savoia €€€€ *Piazza della Repubblica 17; Tel. 02/62301; fax 02/6595838; <www.luxurycollection.com>.* Now combined with the Duke next door, this top-of-the-line hotel right down the street from the station offers all modern comforts in a grand, 19th-century-style décor. 399 rooms.

Sempione €€ *Via Finocchiaro Aprile 11; Tel. 02/6570323; fax 02/6575379.* A quiet and friendly establishment located north of the center. There is an on-site restaurant and the hotel is known to accept small pets. 43 rooms.

Spadari al Duomo €€€ *Via Spadari 11; Tel. 02/72002371; fax 02/861184; <www.spadarihotel.com>.* Clever, modern design with a careful and refined attention to detail; close to cathedral. Closed at Christmas. 40 rooms.

Sunset City Hotel €€€ *Via G. Colombo, 14; Tel. 02/70109561; fax 02/76110496.* A bit out of the way, but worth it for the value. Purely bio-ecological. 12 rooms.

Valley € *Via Soperga 19; Tel. 02/6692777; fax 02/66987252.* Modern, quiet and clean establishment near the railway station with television and parking available. 12 rooms.

BERGAMO

Miralago € *Via 4 Novembre 12; Tel./fax 035/968008; <www.hotel-miralago.com>.* Just a short distance out of town, this hotel-restaurant offers tennis, a wooded park, and a view of Lake Iseo. 45 rooms.

L'Excelsior San Marco €€€ *Piazza della Republica 6; Tel. 035/366111;fax035/223201,email <info@hotelsanmarco.com>.* Modern sleek hotel with roof garden just 5 minutes from the center. Amenities such as in-room fax and jaccuzi. 163 rooms.

BRESCIA

Park Hotel Ca'Noa €€ *Via Triumplina 66; Tel. 030/398762;fax030/398764; email <hotelcanoa@tin.it>.*

Modern elegance in a quiet garden setting on city outskirts; swimming pool, health club, sauna. 78 rooms.

Vittoria €€€ *Via 10 Giornate 20; Tel. 030/280061; fax 030/280065; <www.hotelvittoria.com>*. Comfortable, stylish Neo-Classical 1930s-style hotel with restaurant in the historic city center. 66 rooms.

MONZA

De la Ville €€€ *Viale Regina Margherita 15; Tel. 039/382581; fax 039/367647; <www.delaville.com>*. Directly in front of the Villa Reale park, this lodging offers a peaceful place for Grand Prix fans to relax. Sauna and pool facilities available. Closed August and Christmas. 62 rooms.

PAVIA

Moderno €€ *Viale Vittorio Emanuele 41; Tel. 0382/303401; fax 0382/25225; email <moderno@hotelmoderno.it>*. Simple rustic furnishings allow for a comfortable, unpretentious elegance; close to Pavia's railway station. Closed one week in August and at Christmas. 54 rooms.

VARESE

Motor Hotel Varese Lago €€ *Via Macci 61; Tel. 0332/310022; fax 0332/312687; <www.hotelvareselago.com>*. One of Italy's ever-growing sector of "motels". This one is convenient, just off the highway and 4 km (2.5 miles) from the centre. With more character than most, it offers a pool, gym, Turkish baths, and beauty centre. 44 rooms.

LAKE MAGGIORE

Bristol €€€ *Corso Umberto 73, Stresa; Tel. 0323/32601; fax 0323/33622; <www.grandhotelbristol.com>*. Lakeside hotel with luxurious rooms facing the gardens or the lake, it has the only indoor pool in town. Outdoor pool and lakeside watersports as well. Closed mid-November through February. 270 rooms.

Grand Hôtel des Iles Borromées €€€€ *Corso Umberto 67, Stresa; Tel. 0323/30431; fax 0323/32405; <www.borromees.it>*. A grand monument among resort hotels since 1861, set in a superb lakefront parkland. Every modern comfort, tennis, golf, sauna and two swimming pools. 180 rooms.

Rigoli € *Via Piave 48, Baveno; Tel. 0323/924756; fax 0323/925156.* Small, peaceful hotel with a terrace garden and lakefront views of the Borromean Islands with its own private beach. Convenient location for cruises located north of Stresa. 31 rooms.

Verbano €€ *Isola Pescatori, Via Ugo Ara 2, (Borromean Islands); Tel. 0323/30408 fax 0323/33129; email <hotelverbano@gse.it>*. Guests find peace and tranquillity on this small island and enjoy summer meals on the popular panoramic terrace. Jet skis available to rent. Closed Jan–Feb. 12 rooms.

Villaminta €€€ *Via Nazionale del Sempione 123, Stresa; Tel.0323/933818;fax 0323/933955; <www.stresa.net/hotelvillaminta>*. North of town, offering lakefront panoramas of the Borromean Islands and overflowing flower garden views. Tennis, swimming pool and private beach. Closed from November through March. 68 rooms.

LAKE COMO

Barchetta Excelsior €€€ *Piazza Cavour 1, Como; Tel. 031/3221;fax 031/302622; email <inf.2@hotelbarchetta.com>*. Facing the lake and near the cathedral, with a respected in-house restaurant. Specialized rooms i.e., with jacuzzi or fax meet individualized needs. 84 rooms.

Belvedere € Via Valassina 31, Bellágio; Tel. 031/950410; fax 031/950102; email <belveder@tin.it>. View of Lake Como, and outdoor swimming pool. Terrace sloping directly down to lake.

Closed mid-October to April. Conveniently northeast of Como. 69 rooms.

Grand Hôtel Villa d'Este €€€€ *Via Regina 40, Cernobbio; Tel. (031)3481; fax (031)348844; <www.villadeste.it>.* Palatial resort-hotel, one of the world's finest; 16th-century villa in flowering lakefront gardens. All amenities such as golf, tennis, squash, three swimming pools, watersports and excellent restaurants. Closed from December to February. 158 rooms.

Il Griso €€ *Via Provinciale 51, Malgrate; Tel. 0341/202040; fax 0341/202248; email <hgriso@cot.it>.* Charming modern comfort in delightful lakeside setting. Swimming pool, watersports and gourmet restaurant. South of Lecco. 47 rooms.

Grand Hotel Tremezo €€€€ *località Tremezzo, Como; Tel. 0344/ 42491; fax 0344/40201.* Grand furnishings in a 19th-century-style villa. A groomed lakefront park includes tennis, heated swimming pool and private parking. Closed Dec–Feb. 98 rooms.

Tre Re € *Via Boldoni 20, Como; Tel. 031/265374; fax 031/241349; email <trere@tin.it>.* Quiet, convenient location near the cathedral. Simple but reliably clean. Closed at Christmas. 41 rooms.

Villa Flori €€€ *Via Cernobbio 12, Como; Tel. 031/33820; fax 031/570379; email <lariovillaflori@galatica.it>.* Situated west of town, with lakefront gardens and mountain backdrop. Closed Dec–Feb. 45 rooms.

LAKE GARDA

Astoria Lido € *Via Benaco 20, Sirmione; Tel. 030/9904392; fax 030/9906818; email <info@astorialido.it>.* Friendly family-run hotel with garden and tasteful rooms. Closed from 15 Oct–Easter. 22 rooms.

Coste € *Via Tamas 11, Limone; Tel. 0365/954042; fax 0365/954393; email <hotelcoste@hotelcoste.com>.* Quaint rooms with a private pool and an olive grove behind. Parking available. Closed November and December. 30 rooms.

Grand Hotel Fasano €€€€ *Corso Zanardelli 190, Fasano, Gardone Riviera; Tel. 0365/290220; fax 0365/290221; email <info@grand-hotel-fasano.it>*. An old Hapsburg hunting lodge situated in a beautiful lakeside park. Tennis, swimming pool and beach. Closed mid-October–April. 75 rooms.

Ideal €€ *Via Catullo 31, Sirmione; Tel./fax 030/9904245.* Quaint private hotel with an olive grove that slopes down to the lake. Closed November–April. 33 rooms.

Ilma € *Via Caldogno 1, Limone; Tel. 0365/954041; fax 0365/954535.* A simple hostelry located in a pretty spot with views of both the lake and the mountains. Parking and private restaurant. Closed November–March. 54 rooms.

Laurin €€€€ *Viale Landi 9, Salò; Tel. 0365/22022; fax 0365/22382; email <laurinbs@tin.it>*. Elegant, Liberty-style villa with frescoed salons and a garden-surrounded pool. Full watersport facilities. Closed 1 Dec– 20 Feb. 38 rooms.

Park Hotel Imperial €€€ *via Tamas 10/b, Limone; Tel. 0365/954591; fax 0365/954382; email <imperialcentrotao@telmec.it>*. Italian resort with Eastern-influenced spa treatments. Garden with pool, gym, and tennis. Closed 11–22 Dec. 56 rooms.

Villa del Sogno €€€-€€€€ *Via Zanardelli 107, Fasano, Gardone Riviera; Tel. 0365/290181; fax 0365/290230.* A former villa-turned hotel with grand lakeside gardens, tennis, sauna and pool. Closed mid-October to April. 35 rooms.

Villa Fiordaliso €€ *Via Zanardelli 150, Gardone Riviera; Tel. 0365/20158; fax 0365/290011.* Intimate, historic, and luxurious Belle Epoque villa with well-known gourmet restaurant. Summer terrace park directly on the lake. Closed 20 Nov–10 Feb. 7 rooms.

Recommended Restaurants

Nothern Italian cusine is identified by its butter, cream and cheeses from the mountains; rice and polenta from the plains. Look for these ingredients mixed with other regional specialties in any pizzeria, trattoria, osteria or ristorante listed below. When possible make reservations, since frequent trade shows fill up even out-of-the-way eateries. Join up with the locals for a lunch-time stop in a paninoteca for a tasty sandwich , or in a casual bar for a simple bite, then enjoy a splurge on a fabulous dinner.

Closing days vary, especially in the smaller lake towns. In Milan, Sunday is the usual *giorno di riposo* or day of rest. Resort towns tend to close down in the winter and Milan during the month of August, so your selection will be limited during those periods. Pricing is generally higher in Milan than outside, but you can always be price conscious and eat well at the same time by ordering wisely.

The following categories cover a three-course meal, cover, and service charges, but not wine or any gratuities. Ranges are given as guides only.

€	below €15
€€	€15–30
€€€	€30–50
€€€€	above €50

CENTRAL MILAN

Al Cantinone €€ *Via Agnello 19; Tel. 02/86461338; fax 02/86462898.* Comfortable family-run restaurant featuring a bountiful antipasto selection, Tuscan specialties, and Milanese favorites, both fish and meat. All desserts are produced in-house. Adjoining bar offers convenient stand-up lunch service. Major credit cards; closed Saturday afternoons and Sundays.

Bagutta €€€ *Via Bagutta 14; Tel. 02/76002767; fax 02/799613; <www.bagutta.it>.* Colorful and well-known trattoria where the first Italian literary prize was born and is still bequeathed annually. Enjoy a savory plate of rigatoni alla Bagutta or freshwater fish in the garden (weather permitting) while rubbing elbows with a famous soccer player or reclusive painter. Major credit cards; closed Sundays, most of August, and Christmas.

Bice €€€ *Via Borgospesso 12; Tel. 02/76002572; fax 02/76013356.* Menu comprised of Milanese and Tuscan specialties, from white truffle specialties in season to homemade pasta. This longtime popular spot for the fashion world spawned several Bice siblings in a number of international cities. Major credit cards; closed Mondays, August and 24 December–6 January.

Panino Giusto € *Piazza Beccaria 4, Tel. 02/76005015.* One of four locations in Milan displaying the crest of the Earl of Sandwich at the entrance, assuring the quality of their tasty *panini* (sandwiches). Vegetarians will have no problem here and desserts promise a filling yet inexpensive meal. No credit cards; open until 1am; closed Sundays.

Peck €€€–€€€€ *Via Victor Hugo 4; Tel./fax 02/876774; email <cracco-peck@peck.it>.* Just renovated from top to bottom, including the addition of a celebrated new chef. Very chic atmosphere offering a quick-paced business lunch, and a fixed and à la carte dinner menu offering creative twists on classic

Italian dishes. Distinguished wine cellar contains more than 1,700 international labels. Major credit cards; closed Sundays and first three weeks of July.

NORTH OF CENTRE

Alfredo-Gran San Bernardo €€€ *Via Borgese 14; Tel. 02/3319000; fax 02/6555413.* This is a popular and reliable place to order classic Milanese dishes. Try the *risotto milanese*, *cotolette alla milanese*, and the *cazzoeula*, a pork and cabbage stew served over a bed of polenta. No credit cards; closed Sundays, 20 December–20 January, and mid-July through August.

Al Girarrosto da Cesarina €€€€ *Corso Venezia, 31; Tel. 02/76000481.* A classic Milanese choice known for the house specialty of *polpetone* (a single, oversized meatball) made with Mamma's recipe. Grilled meat or fish in simple Tuscan style are the entrées of choice for the top fashion models who dine here. Great desserts made in-house. Major credit cards; closed Saturdays and Sunday at lunch, August, last week of December, and first week of January.

Antica Trattoria della Pesa €€€ *Viale Pasubio 10; Tel. 02/ 6555741; fax 02/29005157.* Family trattoria serving traditional Lombard cooking. Try the *riso al salto*, a crispy pancake of rice lightly fried in butter — very Milanese, very good. Major credit cards; closed Sundays and all holidays.

Cuccuma € *Via Pacini 26; Tel. 02/2663860.* Pleasant Neapolitan trattoria behind main station. Typical southern fare served in a cozy atmosphere. Try the fried potato croquets, a simple but tasty specialty. No credit cards; closed Tuesdays and Sunday lunch.

Insalatiera delle Langhe €€ Corso Como 6; Tel. 02/ 6595180, fax 02/29006859. Casual salad bar offering more than twenty light lunch, dinner, or late-night options. Possibility of ordering hot dishes from their adjoining

Piemontese (and more formal) dining room. Major credit cards; closed Sundays.

SOUTH AND WEST AND EAST OF CENTRE

Aimo e Nadia €€€€ *Via Montecuccoli 6; Tel. 02/416886; fax 02/48302005.* Well worth the cab ride and the splurge, this husband-and-wife team has created a legend in Milanese (and Italian) dining. Only the best seasonal local produce finds its way to their daily menu featuring both fish and meat cooked with delicateness and finesse. An impressive local cheese selection and excellent wine list make for a unique experience. American Express only; closed Saturday lunch, Sundays, and August.

Da Giacomo €€-€€€ *Via Sottocorno 6; Tel. 02/76023313.* Charming setting for a Tuscan menu featuring seafood. Order porcini mushrooms in season, homemade pasta stuffed with various shellfish, and the grilled catch of the day. Major credit cards; closed Mondays.

Pizzeria Il Mozzo € *Via Ravizzi 1 Tel. 02/4984676.* Authentic Neapolitan pizza baked personally for you in a wood-burning oven. Other dishes are available, but this thick-crusted plateful will make the perfect simple meal. No credit cards; closed Wednesdays, August.

NAVIGLI (CANAL DISTRICT)

El Brellin €€€ *Lavandai Alzaia Naviglio Grande 14; Tel. 02/58101351; fax 02/89402700.* Charming terraced café with a fixed price menu of L70.000 without beverages; live piano on Saturdays. Sunday brunch. Named in dialect after the washboards used in the canal alongside the restaurant where housewives once came to launder. Major credit cards, no American Express; closed Sunday dinner and August.

Posto di Conversazione €€ *Alzaia Naviglio Grande 6; Tel./fax 02/58106646.* An old-time characteristic canal-district trattoria. Seasonal specialties, with menu that changes daily from meat to fish to vegetarian selections. A great dish for two or more is the seabream baked inside a loaf of bread. Major credit cards; always open.

Scaletta €€€€ *Piazzale Stazione Genova 3; Tel./fax 02/58100290; <www.ristorantescaletta.it>.* Creative haute cuisine with both à la carte and degustazione menu. Focused on fish, the *tortino di polipo* featuring octopus is a favourite. Lovely alfresco garden dining in season. Major credit cards; closed Sundays, two weeks in August.

BERGAMO

Da Vittorio €€€€ *Viale Papa Giovanni XXIII 21, Città Bassa; Tel. 035/213266; fax 035/210805.* Considered to be one of Italy's leading restaurants, serving regional specialities in grand style. Try seasonal scampi carpaccio with onion purée or crispy suckling pig. Major credit cards; closed Wednesdays and August.

Marianna €€€ *Largo Colle Aperto 4, Città Alta; Tel. 035/247997; fax 035/211314; email <mirko.panettone-@tin.it>.* Choose from the delightful summer terrace or the 1950s décor dining room. Enjoy local game, fish and white truffle ravioli in season. The owners operate the popular pasticceria below, so don't pass on the exquisite desserts. Major credit cards; closed Mondays.

Musicanti €€€€ *Via San Vigilio 15, Città Alta; Tel. 035/253179; <www.sanvigillo.it>.* This family-run hotel/restaurant is small and reservations are understandably hard to come by. Traditional pasta and seafood dishes are augmented by the daily creative whims of the chef and owner, both an artist and a poet. Enjoy dining on the alfresco terrace in warm months. Major credit cards; closed Tuesdays.

Taverna del Colleoni €€€ *Piazza Vecchia 7; Tel. 035/232596; fax 035/2331991.* Elegant dining room with vaulted ceilings in a Bramante palace. Local fare often features the market's fresh fish for the day, following selections of homemade pasta. Not-to-be-missed desserts should be enjoyed at piazza-side tables, weather permitting. Major credit cards; closed Mondays.

Trattoria del Teatro €-€€ *Piazza Mascheroni 3; Tel./fax 035/238862.* This family-run trattoria serves typical local fare, and is particularly proud of its *cassoncelli* (a type of ravioli) and *faggiano brassato* (braised pheasant) with polenta. No credit cards; closed Mondays.

MONZA

Derby Grill €€€ *Viale Regina Margherita 15; Tel. 039/382581;fax039/367647; email <info@hoteldelaville.com>.* Dine while surrounded by antiques, and enjoy dishes that focus on meat or fish prepared in classic Lombard style. Excellent service and fine wine selection. Major credit cards; closed Saturday lunch, Sundays, 24 December–6 January, and all of August.

PAVIA

Al Cassinino €€€€ *Via Cassinino 1; Tel./fax 0382/422097.* Stylish restaurant, off the main road from Certosa, serving varied poultry and seafood menu as well as homegrown vegetables. Limited seating and always busy. No credit cards; closed Wednesdays.

Antica Osteria del Previ €€ *Via Milazzo 65, località Borgo Ticino; Tel. 0382/26203.* A long-time favorite stopover for businessmen coming and going to and from Milan that has maintained its friendly service. Dig into a bowl of homemade soup, polenta, or deer simmered in red wine. Major credit cards, no American Express; closed lunch in July, August, and 1–10 January.

VARESE

Teatro €€€ *Via Croce 3; Tel. 0332/241124, fax 0332/280994.* Elegant and conveniently located right in the old town centre, serving classic fare. For a twist on risotto, here it is served inside a bowl of homemade bread. Major credit cards; closed Tuesdays and August.

LAKE MAGGIORE

Campanile €€ *Via Montegrappa 16, Baveno; Tel./fax 0323/922377.* Classic pasta dishes in a charming old house situated just north of Stresa. The menu changes monthly according to season. Do not miss the homemade apple strudle. Major credit cards; open daily.

Da Cesare €€€ *Via Mazzini 14, Stresa; Tel. 0323/31386; fax 0323/933810; <www.dacesere.com>.* A family-run operation, set back from the lake in the historic centre of town. In a classic setting, diners can enjoy today's fresh catch from the lake, but the restaurant also serves hearty dishes with lamb, porcini mushrooms and rabbit. Outside seating is available during warm months. Major credit cards, closed on Tuesdays in the winter.

Rigoli € *Via Piave 48, Baveno; Tel. 0323/924756; fax 0323/925156; <www.hotelrigoli.com>.* Local recipes using both freshwater fish and finds from the surrounding forest. Part of a private hotel that enjoys a peaceful location, the kitchen is also known for desserts made in-house. Major credit cards; open daily.

Verbano €€ *Isola dei Pescatori (Borromean Islands); Tel. 0323/30408; fax 0323/33129; <www.hotelverbano.it>.* Elegant setting popular for its terrace dining with spectacular views of Isola Bella. Begin with an appetizer of fresh bass-stuffed ravioli and wind up with a dessert made in the on-site bakery. Major credit cards.

LAKE COMO

Al Giardino €€–€€€ *Via Montegrappa 52, Como; Tel. 031/265016; fax 031/300143.* Elegant garden villa sets the mood for an osteria-style meal of fresh catch from the lake. Small and friendly. Ask the staff to suggest the best dish of the day. Major credit cards; closed Mondays, January, and the second half of August.

Brienno €€€ *Crotto dei Platani, Brienno; Tel./fax 031/814038; <www.crottodeiplatani.it>.* A rustic dining room in a romantic corner of the lake. A friendly staff will recommend from their daily menu, which offers pasta and a wide variety of fresh water fish. Major credit cards; closed Tuesdays and Wednesday lunch.

Busciona € *Via Valassina, Bellagio; Tel./fax 031/964831; <www.vademecumitalia.com/labusciona>.* Friendly trattoria serving both fish and meat, with a fabulous lake view. In the winter, look for braised wild goat served with polenta. Major credit cards; closed Mondays and October.

Il Griso €€€€ *Via Provinciale 51, Malgrate Tel. 0341/202040; fax 0341/202248; email <hgriso@cot.it>.* Highly rated restaurant, part of a charming hotel. Creative cuisine that utilizes local and other regional ingredients. Their special version of risotto is enriched with goose liver and seasoned with rosemary and pesto. Located south of Lecco. Major credit cards.

Porticciolo €€€ *Via Valsecchi 5/7, Lecco; Tel. 0341/498103; fax 0341/258438.* Romantic fireside dinners in winter, garden dining in summer. Purely seafood menu, although vegetarians will be satisfied as well. Major credit cards; dinner only, closed Mondays and Tuesdays.

Sant'Anna 1907 €€€ *Via Turati 3, Como; Tel./fax 031/505266; <santanna.1907@tin.it>.* Intimate atmosphere with fine service and refined variations on local traditions. Apart from freshwater fish, you can find great veal and rabbit. Major credit cards; closed Saturday lunch, Sundays and August.

LAKE GARDA

Alla Campagnola €€ *Via Brunati 11, Salò; Tel. 0365/22153.* Family service and simple preparations render this locale a great find and always full. Outdoor dining, weather permitting. Major credit cards; closed Wednesday lunch and from 15 December–10 February.

Antica Trattoria delle Rose €€–€€€ *Via Gasparo da Salò 33, Salò; Tel./fax 0365/43220.* Here you are greeted by a rustic setting and the anticipation of a wide selection of tasty antipasti. The local fish is prepared with a creative flair here. Major credit cards; closed Wednesdays and November.

Capriccio €€€ *Piazza San Bernardo 6, Montinelle, Manerba; Tel./fax 0365/551124; email <ilcapriccio@-phoenix.it>.* Delightful lakeside terrace for summer service. Specialties of the house include the tagliatelle with scampi or the scallops with pan-roasted vegetables—both are well worth a try. Major credit cards; closed Tuesdays and January–February.

Castello Malvezzi €€€ *Via Colle San Giuseppe 1, Desenzano del Garda; Tel. 030/2004224; fax 030/2004208.* Set in a 16th-century castle, this friendly spot serves creative freshwater fish dishes. Look for a mixed fish shish kebab or half-moon-shaped ravioli dressed with oysters and fresh tomatoes. Major credit cards; closed Mondays, Tuesdays, January and throughout August.

Esplanade €€€–€€€€ *Via Lario 10, Desenzano del Garda; Tel./fax 030/9143361.* Highly acclaimed establishment in a quaint lakeside garden setting, you can find unusual items on the menu such as eel and white bait among the less esoteric dishes. Winter menus feature pumpkin and radicchio in various combnations. Major credit cards; closed Wednesdays and major holidays.

Gallo Rosso €€ *Vicolo Tolacelli 4 Salò;* Tel. 0365/520757. Great quality for your money. Relaxed atmosphere serving local comfort food, including seafood, pasta and risotto. Wines are included in the budgeted range of this family locale. Major credit cards; closed Wednesdays, 7–14 January and 25 June–5 July.

Lorenzaccio €€€ *Via Cipro 78, Brescia; Tel. 030/220457; fax 030/2479834.* A welcoming family restaurant specializing in meat dishes. Look for polenta dishes and a number of dishes enriched by creamy taleggio cheese. Major credit cards; closed Saturday nights, 23 December–10 January, August, and weekends in June and July.

Piazzetta €€€ *Via Indipendenza 87c, Sant'Eufemia della Fonte, Desenzano del Garda; Tel./fax 030/362668; <www.allapiazzetta.com>.* Small restaurant seating 35 in Liberty-style décor. Although they are on the lake, you will find many sea specialities as well. Look for pasta with shell-fish and desserts made in-house. Major credit cards; closed Saturday lunch, Sundays, first week of January, and two weeks in August.

La Sosta €€€€ *Via San Martino della Battaglia 20, Brescia; Tel. 030/295603, fax 030/292589.* Set in 17th-century Palazzo Martinengo delle Palle; a beautiful backdrop for an exquisite meal. Try whole grilled fish or homemade pasta sauced with tiny clams. Major credit cards; closed Sunday dinner, Mondays, 1–8 January and 6–28 August.

Tortuga €€€€ *Via XXIV Maggio 5, Gargnano; Tel. 0365/71251; fax 0365/71938.* Highly recommended for its elegant setting and menu full of precious delicacies. Here they use the very finest of local produce and freshwater fish. Major credit cards; closed Tuesdays, Mondays in the off season, during Christmas, and 15 January–1 March.

INDEX